Acknou

Elizabeth Clamon is a gifted natural health provider who understands the mind-body-spirit connection so well. This book helps you understand why, as she shares her personal journey from brokenness to wholeness. It is no easy task to travel that road. It takes great courage and perseverance, but her story inspires and challenges everyone struggling with a painful past to summon the courage to follow her example.

—Kathy Barton - Clinical Social Worker

Beauty Rising from Brokenness is a story very close to my own heart. The author, Elizabeth M. Clamon, does an amazing job at, not only sharing her story, but explaining how the feelings, emotions and brokenness can be transferred from life to life. I love the transparency. I can feel the resilience and determination, in every scenario, as I read the story. If you have every questioned brokenness in your life, need to know if you are dealing with someone who is broken or need to overcome the spirit of brokenness, this book is a must read.

—Precious S. Brown CEO|Founder Precious Empowers Enterprise Amazon International Bestselling Author, The Business Liaison for New Mompreneurs, www.buildingbusinessbasics101.com

Chronic pain is a completely consuming condition with lasting and detrimental effects. Elizabeth Clamon, through her book Beauty Rising from Brokenness, shows how there is an alternative from suffering through your own personal, and possibly painful, circumstances. Elizabeth provides her unique perspective of childhood abuse and chronic pain intertwined with her experience as a Natural Health Provider for practical approaches to living with your unexpected issues. This is a great resource for anyone who is seeking wholeness in the midst of a broken life.

—Eric Eaton Author of The Raging Sloth and The Thrival Guide.

"… a totally engrossing, interesting book that will have you turning pages quickly as Elizabeth takes you through her journey, from broken to healed, from despair to happiness enlightenment and joy. She will help you begin your own journey of healing, no matter where you are in that process. This is a must-read for anyone who's been through trauma, who feels lost or who is truly broken. There is hope, and Beauty Rising from Brokenness is the answer."

—Lee Tkachuk, Award-Winning CEO,
Best-Selling Author, Professional Speaker, and
Founder of The Speaker Collaborative

Also by Elizabeth Clamon

Remember the Butterfly effect? Everything effects everything; How Stress Affects your Health

20 Chronic Illnesses and their Natural Healing Therapies

Voices of the 21ˢᵗ Century: Women Who Influence, Inspire, and Make a Difference

I RISE: Living Beyond the Bruises Anthology December 2018

Beauty Rising from Brokenness:

Journey through Childhood Trauma and Chronic Illness into Healing

Faith Radio Listener,
Be Blessed and Be a Blessing

Elizabeth M. Clamon

Elizabeth Clamon

Based on a True Story

Roman 8:28

AUTHOR ACADEMY elite

Paperback: 978-1-64085-444-4

Hardback: 978-1-64085-445-1

Ebook: 978-1-64085-446-8

Library of Congress Control Number (LCCN): 2018957229

Dedication

For my family, Kathy, and God without them I would never have survived this journey. My husband Arnold for his unconditional love and unwavering support. My children Megan, Brittney, and Joshua, I'm sorry you had to go through this, but your all strong, loving, and compassionate people and better for it, I believe. Your love and support mean more to me than you will ever know. To Kathy, my counselor, confidant, and friend for your guidance and love while walking with me down this long and difficult path. God, my Abba (Daddy)," For ye have not received the spirit of bondage again to fear; but ye have received the Spirit of adoption, whereby we cry, Abba, Father." (Romans 8:15 KJV) your great love, your Word, loving me enough to send your only son to die for me," For God so loved the world, that he gave his only begotten Son, that whosoever believeth in him should not perish, but have everlasting life." (John 3:16 KJV) and your Spirit who comforted and interceded when I was so broken I couldn't even pray." Likewise, the Spirit also helpeth our infirmities: for we know not what we should pray for as we ought: but the Spirit itself maketh intercession for us with groanings which cannot be uttered." (Romans 8:26 KJV)

A joyful heart is good medicine, But a broken spirit dries up the bones (Proverbs 17:22 NASB)

Table of Contents

Part 1: HARDSHIP – The Why

Brokenness, How Did I Get Here?
   Are you Broken?

Part 2: HURT – The How

The First Major Crack
   Do you have fractures?

The Brokenness Begins to Affect Me Physically
   Are you suffering from chronic illness?

Foreword

I grew up hearing the saying that "the truth will make you free." I believe my parents quoted the phrase because they believed I had done something wrong, i.e., left food out on the kitchen counter or accidentally missed the trash can while tossing some trash. Nothing major, but they were certainly looking for a confession from me. Naturally, I wasn't a liar, so I would confess, only when it was applicable. But I still didn't have an appreciation for the statement, "the truth will make you free."

My appreciation for the truth came because of growing up in my local church and witnessing what was then called, "testimony service." It was a time in the just before an official service; bible study typically, and before the choir would sing. But the moderator of the church service would ask if anyone in the congregation had a testimony they wanted to share. Often people would stand up and share something that may not have been relevant to me. However, every now and again, someone would share their testimony about a personal experience or encounter that caused them to change their lives for the better.

No solicited or forced confessing from Elizabeth M. Clamon.

"Beauty Rising from Brokenness: Journey through Childhood Trauma and Chronic Illness into Healing" is Elizabeth M. Clamon's relevant testimony. Her story is one that demonstrates the power of trusting the God in you, making a conscious decision, and taking necessary action. Elizabeth's story is one that I longed to hear during testimony service that would stir my soul, bring tears to my eyes, and cause me to be introspective.

Elizabeth shares her truth in such a profoundly open and honest way that by the time you finish reading "Beauty Rising from Brokenness: Journey through Childhood Trauma and Chronic Illness into Healing," you will experience the same freedom she has come to know firsthand. You will laugh. You will cry. You will hold your breath, and sigh breaths of relief. You will want to live your life for the better.

Elizabeth is both entertaining and inspiring. I had the pleasure of interviewing Elizabeth on my television/radio program. We clicked instantly because of her authentic bare-her-soul approach to life and serving others. She's made it her life's mission to help others live a life of freedom by living their truth, on their terms. She is a bold force to be reckoned with and well equipped, both experientially and academically. She is empowered to not only help others but also make a difference in the world.

Ready or not, Elizabeth M. Clamon's testimony of transition from being broken to wholeness in "Beauty Rising from Brokenness: Journey through Childhood Trauma and Chronic Illness into Healing" will bless you, spirit, soul, and body.

Let the journey begin!

Dr. Lisa Lewis Ellis
CEO & Founder Kick Boxing Believers, L.L.C.
John Maxwell Certified Coach, Speaker, Teacher, and Trainer
https://www.johncmaxwellgroup.com/lisaellis/

Introduction

What we fear doing most is usually what we
most need to do."—Tim Ferriss

I am *Broken*!! It hit me like a ton of bricks. I was waking up to
the fact that I was broken and probably always had been. What
was broken? What would it be like to be unbroken? When did
the brokenness start? How did I get this way? How did I become
broken? Who or what broke me in the first place?

I had no idea. As I stood staring out the door of our new
home in Michigan, the snow blew in drifts, it felt like the cold
wind was blowing through the huge cracks in my soul.

I didn't know what to do or where to turn for help, I just
wanted to disappear. Not from life but from my brokenness. I felt
like an injured animal. I wanted to crawl in as small of a place
as I could find and heal. The only problem, I didn't know how.
I was the mother of three young children. My military husband
had deployed just three months after we moved to this cold and
lonely place. I had to stay out in the open, I had to try to live
despite the gut-wrenching pain and brokenness.

In *Beauty Rising from Brokenness* I will tell you how I became broken and how I found my way back to hope and healing. Do I still have cracks, yes? But now there is a bright, beautiful light that shines through my cracks where there once was anger, rage, sadness, depression, illness, and pain.

Are you broken? Do you know? Do you feel like you have cracks that go all the way to the core of your very being? Do you want to run away, to escape the pain, to find a small, still, place where you can heal? Most of us have families, jobs, friends, and all sorts of other people who need us, who depend on us, and running to a safe place to heal simply isn't doable. So, what do you do? What did I do? I will guide you down the path I took to healing in this book.

I have walked this path of brokenness for most of my life. The journey was long and difficult. Being on the other side now. I realize how incredibly hard, yet worthwhile the trek was. I wrote this book because I've traveled this path and I know how long, lonely, and difficult it is. Also. I have studied Naturopathic medicine, so I can guide you in a way few others can. "Naturopathic medicine is a distinct primary health care method, emphasizing prevention, treatment, and optimal health using therapeutic methods and substances that encourage individuals' inherent self-healing process. The practice of Naturopathic medicine includes modern and traditional, scientific, and empirical methods." (1)

It was very important to me to heal naturally. I had been sick my entire life and it seemed all traditional western medicine had done was run down my body and make me worse, as I continued to seek out their treatments. I decided it was time for me to find a different way to heal so I pursued healing through natural means.

For me this meant following the principals that are the foundation of Naturopathic Medicine. There are five therapeutic principles found in Naturopathy.

1. Nature is a powerful healing force - this is the belief that the body has considerable power to heal itself.

2. The person is viewed as a whole - Understanding that a person is an individual is essential.

3. The goal is to identify and address the cause of the problem - Naturopathy does not deal in suppressing symptoms, since symptoms are expression of the body's attempt to heal itself.

4. The Naturopath is a teacher - First and foremost the Naturopath is a teacher, educating, empowering, and motivating the client to assume more personal responsibility for their own wellness by adopting a healthy attitude, lifestyle, and diet.

5. Prevention is the best approach - Prevention is best accomplished by lifestyle habits which support health. (2)

In this book you will not only learn how we become broken, but how to heal and be whole again. To completely heal and be whole we must achieve balance. To achieve balance, we must heal physically, mentally, emotionally, and spiritually. If one area is out of balance the whole cannot heal. I realized this when I had resolved three areas, but there was still one piece I needed to resolve to heal. Once I completed the very difficult task of facing down that last demon my health began to turn around. It didn't happen overnight, but it did happen for me and it can for you too.

Most of my life I remember always being sick, mostly with upper respiratory illnesses and lots of strep throat as a child. I was constantly taken to doctors and given antibiotics and steroids so that I would be back up as soon as possible. Now with my Naturopathic education I realize that the medication was only wrecking my immune system and setting me up to get sicker as I grew older.

I believe we must heal mentally, emotionally, physically, and spiritually to be whole and enjoy optimal health. Every person is a complex design of interconnected pieces. Every part affects all the fragments of the whole being. Western medicine splits us up into parts and just takes care of a problem in one area, never considering that every part is interconnected. We need to consider the whole person and realize that for example, physical pain can be caused by an emotional issue.

Deep emotional and spiritual wounds never heal if you cover them up with a bandage. Often, we try to hide them under a covering of humor, sarcasm, pretending, or self-hatred. This never heals, it only allows the wounds to fester until they are so infected the healing takes a very long time or destroys us from the inside out. Those traumas need to be out in the open to heal. It's always better to get those things out as soon as possible, so the process is easier and faster.

When you finish this book, you will identify the traumas that lead to your brokenness and how each area affects the whole. I will guide you down the path to healing the brokenness. You will know how each part of our being is intricately connected and begin the work of healing each area as we travel the path to healing and freedom.

The longer you wait to begin the journey the more layers get added on to those gaping wounds and harder it will be to heal. If you don't begin to walk the path to hope and healing today, well then when? Ask yourself what you want. Do you want to live with the soul-shattering pain another day or do you want to take the first step to healing? Today is the *best* day to begin. The sooner you start, the closer you are to the finish line. Let's get going. The journey is long and hard, but the freedom at the end is so very worth the relief you feel. What are you waiting for? Let's get stated.

PART 1

HARDSHIP –
The Why

CHAPTER 1

Brokenness, How Did I Get Here? Are you Broken?

I am not a product of my circumstances. I am a
product of my decisions.—Stephen Covey

The song *Broken Things* by Matthew West speaks volumes
to me, because I am one of those "Broken Things." I don't
believe I was whole or unbroken at birth. The circumstances of
my birth were stressful, to say the least, and my beginnings were
humble and disturbing for everyone involved. My birth mother
was under a great deal of stress while she was pregnant with me
and that only multiplied after I was born.

I was a surprise child, as in, no one in my family expected me
until I arrived. My mother says she had no idea she was pregnant.

My family was not only in shock, but ashamed. Being a single mother in 1965 was frowned upon, to say the least. During her pregnancy my mother was going to college, working, and driving home to Louisiana from Mississippi on the weekends. After my birth she had to quit school, go to work, and move back in with my grandparents. That was difficult for everyone and caused a great deal of stress for the entire family.

Many people don't realize how much that stress, both pre-birth and post-birth affects the child. Perhaps as much or more than the adults in the situation. Adults can choose to make changes in their environment, and their thinking. A child, however, has no such choice. We are subject to the choices, feelings, and environment around us. Our brains and bodies adapt and overcome but that's due to our will to survive. We have an innate ability to survive. We want to live. We see this in premature infants that refuse to give up. Against all odds they fight to survive.

That survival instinct is a God-given ability to want to live and go on despite how hard living might be. However, it does take its toll on our brain and body. Those premature babies often have lifelong issues with hearing, vision, learning disabilities, and much more (4), but those of us that are born otherwise healthy don't escape without long-term challenges as well. It is well documented that children born and raised in stressful environments suffer changes in their brain chemistry and body that tend to affect them adversely for life.

In a study of Adverse Childhood Experience (ACE) in Minnesota, "Ongoing adversity in childhood leads to a chronic state of "fight, flight or freeze." Researchers at Yale University discovered that when inflammatory stress hormones flood a child's body and brain, they alter the genes that oversee our stress reactivity, re-setting the stress response to "high" for life." (5) "This increases the risk of inflammation, which manifests later in cancer, heart disease, autoimmune diseases and many other chronic conditions." (6)

"Alters the genes that oversee our stress reactivity, re-setting the stress response to *high* for life." (5) Think about that for a minute, if you're born and/or raised in this type of environment you are altered for the rest of your life. *Wow!* By no choice of your own, the environment makes changes you will deal with forever. You can begin the process of healing by assessing your risk factors by taking the ACE's quiz at ElizabethClamon.com/gift.

Is this fair? No, it's not fair. How many things in life do you know that are? I know from my fifty-two years of experience on this earth, not much has been fair.

So, what about hope? Is there hope? *Yes*, there is always hope. We have hope because God loved us so much he sent Jesus to die for us, so that we can live life in abundance. We often think of abundance being financial, but it is abundance in every area of life, even our health. The verse in the song *Broken Things* by Matthew West says, "The pages of history they tell me it's true, that it's never the perfect; it's always the ones with the scars that You use, It's the rebels and the prodigals; it's the humble and the weak, the misfit heroes You chose, Tell me there's hope for sinners like me" (3)

Sinners like me in the song *Broken Things* refers to the fact that we are all sinners. We are sinners because we are born in a sinful world. This dates to the book of Genesis when Adam and Eve sinned by disobeying God and eating from the tree of knowledge of good and evil.

"And He said, Who told you that you were naked? Have you eaten of the tree of which I commanded you that you should not eat? And the man said, The woman whom You gave to be with me--she gave me [fruit] from the tree, and I ate. And the Lord God said to the woman, What is this you have done." (Genesis 3:11 - 3:13a AMP)

> "The pages of history they tell me it's true
> That it's never the perfect;
> it's always the ones with the scars that You use
> It's the rebels and the prodigals; it's the humble and the weak
> All the misfit heroes You chose
> Tell me there's hope for sinners like me"
> From song Broken Things by Matthew West (3)

The ones with scar that you use, makes perfect sense and the biggest difference in the world. Maybe the challenges also make us strong in other ways, determined to make a change, even rebel against the things that changed us forever. Maybe those changes, while giving us challenges that must be overcome, also gives us a determined spirit to change the world.

That is at least true for me. Despite the circumstances of my birth, the dysfunctional and abusive childhood I endured, made me strong, stubborn, rebellious, and left me with irreversible scars. However, they are scars I'm proud of. I've earned every one of them. Without my scars I have no idea who I would be. The scars have also left their irreversible damage. Despite the difficulties. I refuse to sit on the sidelines and not leave my mark on this world.

When I was born in rural Louisiana, it was a very different time and place. You didn't have babies out of wedlock. If you did become pregnant while unmarried you were sent off to an unwed mothers' home to have the baby, give it up for adoption, and then you were expected to come back home and resume your life like nothing happened. These young women were impacted for life by this experience and their inability to have any say in their life. If they were unmarried, their father was in control; and if married their husband was in control. The stress of not having any say in what happens to you and having no control over your own life also takes a huge toll on the unborn child. A mother under that type of duress, emotionally torn and scared leaves those scars on the soul of her unborn child. Not to mention her fear of childbirth, alone, often with no opportunity to hold or care for her newborn child. This stress transfers to the child and the brokenness begins. (7)

I was not born under all these circumstances, however mine were similar. My mother was nineteen when she became pregnant with me. Somehow, she managed to hide her pregnancy for the entire nine months. She says she did not know she was pregnant and maybe she didn't. I can only draw from the experience of my own five pregnancies and I knew almost immediately something was different with my body. I've always had an innate, God-given ability, to listen and understand what my body is telling me.

Besides my mother being unmarried and pregnant, there had to have been other extenuating circumstances around her during and after her pregnancy. I have asked questions over the years, but to no avail. No one will tell me exactly what was going on in the home at the time. What I have been told was my mother was in secretarial school in Mississippi and working at the public library. This was apparently where she met my biological father.

What I do know is that I have always had extreme feelings of guilt, the need for everyone to be pleased with me, and the fear of abandonment has always been my constant companion. I never remember a time when I haven't felt that way. So why and how does a young child develop feelings like that, when they've never experienced anything to cause them to feel that way? Transfer; Yes, transfer of feelings the mother is experiencing to the child in utero and in those early informative years of growth and development. (7)

What Is Early Trauma?

"It has long been known that nicotine, alcohol, drug use and poor nutrition have traumatic effects on prenates and babies. We are learning that stressful family events, emotional tension and the way routine medical procedures are performed may also have long-lasting traumatic effects. In fact, trauma occurs in many different situations. It can come from something as obvious as being born prematurely or something as subtle as losing a twin in the early stages of fetal development. Early prenatal experiences like a death in the family and not being wanted are significant examples. Likewise, being whisked away from one's parents right after birth can be particularly traumatic, as can interventions like induced labor and birth by caesarian section. The term "birth trauma" specifically refers to adverse experiences one has during birth, but any traumatic events that take place between conception and about the age of three have particular significance in shaping an individual's life." (7) You can find out more in the resources in the Companion Guide at ElizabethClamon.com/gift.

My mother had to have been under extreme stress and huge feelings of guilt, knowing how her parents would react to my birth. Or like she told me, not knowing what was going on until she started having pain so severe she had to be rushed to the hospital where, I made my grand entrance. I know she was shamed, looked down on, and felt terribly guilty when the truth came out. Also, not knowing where my biological father was must have been especially difficult. Once she found him, after my birth, she discovered he was already married and had a child. This discovery took its toll on her. I don't know who she was before, but the woman I knew was broken and has never found healing and freedom.

It seems to me that she allowed her brokenness to destroy her life. The negativity seems to have affected every relationship she has had since. Now she has no contact with my children or me due to it. Her inability to move on is sad and I feel for her, however I will not and cannot have sympathy for her.

Life is about the cards your dealt and what you chose to do with them. Some people take the hand they are dealt and chose to close themselves off emotionally and not even try to get help and healing. Others seem to be able to take the blows life inflicts and pick themselves up and put the pieces back together and keep going.

I am the type of person who took the cards I was dealt and chose to seek out help, because I desperately wanted to be free and healed of my lifelong brokenness. For years I went through life not even knowing why I was the way I was. I was always a people pleaser, had a huge fear of being left or abducted and not knowing how I would get back home, and I always had an overwhelming feeling of being responsible for everything and everyone. I lived my life from these feelings and thought I was functioning. I was attempting to hide it from everyone around me.

PART 2

HURT - The How

CHAPTER 2

The First Major Crack
Do you have fractures?

The most common way people give up their power is
by thinking they don't have any.
—Alice Walker

By the time I was in my thirties, I came to a point that I felt I needed to know where I came from. Up to this point in my life, despite asking repeatedly, no one would tell me who my biological father was. I asked my mother repeatedly growing up and she always became very irrational, emotional, and verbally abusive, so much so, that I finally quit asking.

I did gather up the courage to ask my grandmother once after my oldest daughter was born. She told me she had sworn to my mother that she would never give me his name. I was obviously upset, so she gave me a few facts, I believe in hopes it would pacify my need to know and it did for a while. She told me he was a nice young man, he had been to their home on several occasions for meals and they really liked him. He was a traveling worker of some kind and therefore had an erratic schedule.

She then went on to tell me they had no idea my mother was pregnant until I was born. After I was born my mother went to find him and when she came back, she told my grandmother she found out he was married and had a child. After that they never talked about it again. However, for years around holidays a man would call her home and ask to speak to my mother. My mother always refused to take the call and eventually the calls stopped.

I came to terms, at the time, that this was probably all I would ever know, especially after my grandmother passed away a year later. I really didn't give much thought to who my father was after this. I was so consumed with grief over losing my grandmother, then our second daughter was born just six months later. My husband had joined the Air Force Reserves and was in basic training. Life was just busy and there wasn't time to dwell on who my father might be.

The next ten years went by in the blink of an eye, it seems. We experienced more loss with a second-trimester miscarriage of our third child. Our son was born a couple years later and immediately went into the neonatal unit. Being a third cesarean section for me, he was born with immature lungs and required special care and oxygen in the neonatal unit. My mother, step-dad, and younger brother were there for his birth, but they had made plans to visit my sister and her family in New Orleans that weekend. After they took our son to neonatal I needed the love and support of family.

In my time of great need where was my family? They left and went to New Orleans as they had planned. I can't tell you how much that hurt me, and it revealed yet another crack of my brokenness. The deep-seated feeling of abandonment and being less-than came rushing back. Thank God my in-laws came over from Texas to help and our church family gave us the support and love we desperately needed during this trying time.

Over the course of the next few years we moved from our first home. We had bought near where I spent my teen years.

Six-months after we got married, we bought and cleared a piece of land ourselves and put a modular home on it. It was five minutes from my mom and stepdad. We lived there until the spring of 1997. We loved living out in the country, but the one-hour drive I made to drop our girls at school and go to work began wearing on me greatly. We put that home on the market and prepared to move closer to my job and our girls' school.

We bought a wonderful house that was built in 1922, closer to work and the girls' school. We loved that old house. It was big and had all kinds of character. From the original hardwood floors to twelve-foot ceilings. My husband was working the swing shift at the time and I was working day shift, so our son didn't have to go to daycare. We had been doing this for three years since our son was born and we were getting tired of working opposite schedules.

We were not particularly happy with the experience we were having with our girls in school, so in the spring of 1997 we made the decision for me to quit work, my husband to go back on day shift, and bring our girls home from school to try homeschooling. My in-laws were supportive and happy to help in any way possible, my mom however told me I was crazy. Once again, no support, not even an encouraging word, my brokenness keeps expanding.

As God's timing would have it, just a few months after we made this major change, my husband was selected for Officer Candidate School in the Air Force Reserves. We were elated, but it meant him quitting his full-time job and going to military school in Tennessee. I knew it would be hard, but after much time in prayer we felt it was what we were supposed to do.

I knew the possibility of my family's reaction being the same as always. I would likely have no family to help or back me up and that's exactly what happened. I made it on my own with the help of wonderful Godly friends, but no help from my mom and stepdad at all. My in-laws helped every way they could, coming over on weekends, finances, love and support, but I got none of that from my family.

My mother, stepdad, and brother had moved to Texas a couple years before due to my mother being transferred with her job.

Frankly, when they moved it was a relief not to have them nearby. Being on my own with them hundreds of miles away was better for me. The briefness of our interactions during this time was a sweet relief, we saw them a few times a year when we made the drive to their home or the one time they came to Louisiana. However, for the most part I was on my own while my husband was away in school.

After my husband graduated from officer candidate school we worked hard to provide for our children. We mowed yards, sold firewood, roofed houses, whatever it took to make ends meet on our own, with neither of us having a steady job. My grandmother had shared a Bible verse with me when I was a teenager and I held on to it with all my might during this difficult time., God always provides for our every need if we just trust Him.

"I have learned in any and all circumstances the secret of facing every situation, whether well-fed or going hungry, having a sufficiency and enough to spare or going without and being in want. I have strength for all things in Christ Who empowers me [I am ready for anything and equal to anything] through Him Who infuses inner strength into me; I am self-sufficient in Christ's sufficiency." (Philippians 4:12 - 4:13 AMP)

Our first set of military orders came in the summer of 1998, two months in Florida, Cocoa Beach to be exact. We decided to pack up our camper and go with my husband to Florida. We were supposed to be there for two months, but as life would have it, we stayed in Florida for two years. First a couple of months at a base in Cocoa Beach, then a civilian job in Lake City, then back to Cocoa Beach for a job on base. That's three moves in two years, you would think I didn't have much time to think about my brokenness or contemplate who my father might be or if I would ever know, however those thoughts were my constant companion.

Florida was the first time I had ever lived away from home. I began to feel a sense of freedom I had never known. I also began to look at my life up until this point and realized I still wanted to know, I had this deep-seated, unquenchable thirst to know who my biological father was. I needed to know, to understand, who was he? Who I am? Why wasn't he in my life? Why would no one tell me the truth after thirty plus years?

While we were in Lake City, Florida my sister and her husband were active duty Navy in Hawaii. I had not seen her or my niece in several years, so when I found out they were going to be in Texas for Christmas in 1998 I decided I had to go for a visit. I love my younger siblings so much, in a lot of ways I feel more like a mother to them than a sister. They are nine and thirteen years younger than I. I was responsible for them for much of their childhood, and I love them both dearly, as if they are my own children.

We decided to go to Texas for a visit and see my sister and her family while they were stateside. My husband had only been at his new job a couple months, so it was necessary for the children and I to make the drive to Texas by ourselves. We made the drive in a couple of days, but things at my mother's house were all but joyful or a celebration of Christmas. It was chaos to say the least! My mother and stepdad fighting over every little thing like always, their tiny house chaotic with all the extra people.

After we had been there a few days my husband was flying in from Florida for a week. I had to pick him up at the airport in the middle of the night and my stepdad insisted on driving into the city with me, so he went with me to get my husband from the airport. I thought this was my opportunity. Finally, I could ask him about my biological father and hopefully he would give me the information I needed without me having to ask my mother and risk crossing her again.

Well, when I ask he told me he didn't know. I couldn't believe it, you have been married to this woman for twenty-plus years, raised her child, and you hadn't even asked. I don't know why that surprised me, looking back on it now it makes perfect sense. I don't think my mother has spoken my biological father's name since I was born. My stepdad said he would talk with her about it and see what he could find out for me. I begged him not to say anything until we all went home after Christmas. But oh no He couldn't possibly do that, because like always, if there is an opportunity to stir up trouble he's first in line.

Laying in the room next door, while my husband and children slept, I could hear him in the next room telling my mother our entire conversation and that she needed to answer my questions. As I drifted off into a restless sleep I wondered what tomorrow held. It wouldn't be long until I found out.

I got up the next morning, my children were already up watching cartoons. I knew immediately upon walking into the room that my mother was furious. The air hung thick, heavy with pure anger and rage. I didn't say anything or make eye contact with her, I made a cup of coffee and sat down on the couch. As I sat there drinking my coffee and dreading what I knew inevitably was to come, tears began streaming down my face. As soon as my mother saw my tears, she perceived them as weakness and she pounced. I could feel her cold stare boring into the side of my head, her rage palpable to everyone in the room. I got up and started down the hall back to the room we were staying in, I just needed to feel safe and at that moment, I certainly didn't feel safe in the room with her.

As I got up she finally spoke to me and said, "What the hell is your problem?" my response, "I'm not the one with the problem, you are". The rage and hate were so terrifying, you could feel it in the room like a dark storm brewing on the horizon. Her next comment was, "if you have something to say to me, say it!". My response, "I'm not getting into this here in front of my children", it wasn't something I felt they needed to witness, since it was quite clear my mother was going to make a scene the same way she had all the other times I had asked who my father was. She replied, "then let's go to the back bedroom".

We went into her bedroom, no sooner than the door clicked shut she exploded on me, over thirty years of hate, built up inside her, that was really directed at my biological father, came flying at me like a dormant volcano spewing searing-hot lava. She told me I had no right to ask about him or to know who he was, after all, if he wanted me he would have come to my grandparents' home to meet me. Angry, hurtful, devastating words flew back and forth for an hour or more, until I couldn't take it anymore.

Feeling spent, injured, and exhausted I left her bedroom and went back to the room my family was staying in.

I retrieved our suitcases from the closet and quickly began packing, preparing to leave and go to my in-law's house. At least there I would feel safe, loved, and at peace. Then my husband entered the room, the hours' worth of screaming in the next room had woken him. He had joined the children in the living room, until the storm seemed to have calmed down. He asked what I was doing, I said, "packing to leave, I don't want to be here, any longer." Unfortunately, that wasn't how he saw it, his thoughts were we should stay because the children had so looked so forward to Christmas at their grandparents and spending it with their cousin. I was so shell-shocked I couldn't gather the strength to argue with him, I just said, "ok, but I have to leave for a little while."

After all these years of marriage he knew it wasn't a good idea to argue with me when I was in this state of mind, he also knew my way of calming down and gathering myself was to go for a long drive. I got dressed, he stayed there with the children and I headed to the truck. Unfortunately, my mother was not done with me. She followed me to the truck and asked where I thought I was going, I said "anywhere you are not." Then she proceeded to lay into me again right there in the driveway. Her main concern? Who else had I asked about my biological father, my grandmother, my aunts, uncles? I told her only my grandmother, but she would not give me his name which was all I wanted.

Finally, after struggling to move past her and get in the truck, I managed to drive away. She was still standing in the driveway staring at me with more hatred and anger than I had ever known was possible, especially from a mother to her child. I just wanted, desperately wanted, to find a church to go to, sit in and pray. Every time in my life, when things got tough church was a peaceful place of restoration. Of course, two days before Christmas there were no churches open, every church door I went to was locked and there was no one at any of them to let me in or even to talk to.

My next option, McDonald's drive-thru. I got a cup of coffee and parked under some tress in the back. I knew what I needed was a Jesus infusion, how could I get that in a McDonald's parking lot? Well, as it turned out I had gotten my husband a WOW CD set of Christian music for Christmas and it was still in the back seat wrapped in bright, beautiful, Christmas paper. I was so relieved it hadn't made it into the house and under the tree. I quickly unwrapped it and popped it in the stereo. Thank God I had it, for it brought me a peace I can't get anywhere else but praise and worship music. I must have sat there for hours, several trips through the drive-thru for coffee, just listening to those CD's, praying, and weeping.

When I finally got myself together enough to head back to their house my mother had calmed down, somewhat. I asked my husband later, "What happened while I was gone?" he said, "Nothing." She didn't say anything to anyone, she didn't cry, she just came back in and acted like everything was normal. But me, I was broken-hearted and sinking further into my first bout with serious depression.

I spent the rest of our time there, two more days, avoiding her as much as possible. I stayed in the bedroom, left every chance I got, and kept to myself; a form of self-protection I suppose, one I had learned many years earlier.

The day after Christmas we loaded up the truck and got ready to head out to my in-laws for the rest of our trip. But before I could leave I felt I owed my sister and brother an apology for ruining Christmas for everyone. I wrote my sister a letter that I slipped in her hand as we hugged them goodbye. I just told her how sorry I was about how the holidays had turned out and asked her and my brother not to hate me. I felt as if everything was my fault. Like I had ruined the holidays for everyone. Often children with Adverse Childhood Trauma, (5) who grow up in dysfunctional families feel that everything is somehow their fault, it's a heavy burden to bear.

So, the first major crack in my brokenness was evident to anyone willing to look. My mother-in-law knew immediately when we arrived at their house that something was very wrong, she pressed me to confide in her, reluctantly I did, and it helped to have someone else who cared and who I knew would pray for me. After a few days visiting my husband's family, me just struggling not to fall completely apart, we headed home and for about a month my mother left me alone. It was a welcome relief not to feel obligated to talk to her every week on the phone.

Then one fateful Sunday afternoon she called. This was her practice, call every Sunday afternoon and have a ten-minute conversation so she could pretend she had a relationship with me. I refused to answer the phone, so my husband did. My mother just said, "Well, I guess Elizabeth doesn't want to talk to me." She was right I didn't, but my husband gently insisted that I should, he said, "maybe there's a way to work things out, maybe she called to tell you what you want to know." He said, "She is your mother, you should talk to her". So, I caved and took the phone, nothing was different at all. Things went right back to the same way they had been for years, Sunday afternoon phone calls, me pretending on the phone to be alright, and her making small talk convincing herself nothing had happened, and everything was fine, but I was far from fine.

This continued through the rest of our time in Florida and into our next move to Massachusetts. I lived my life, big cracks in my soul, gaping open, agonizing pain oozing out, but on the outside, I tried to make it look like everything was fine. However, it was taking its toll on me physically. You can only go on for so long with deep cracks all the way to your soul before they begin to affect your physical health and that is exactly what happened to me.

CHAPTER 3

The Brokenness Begins to Affect Me Physically

Are you suffering from chronic illness?

Your body hears everything your mind says.
—Naomi Judd

It began with Asthma, then went into repeat chronic respiratory infections, and bronchitis that I got so many times I could barely walk down the stairs without gasping for breath. I was so exhausted I could barely make it through my day. Every illness that went around I would get it. Emotions that aren't true to yourself begin to take their toll on other parts of the body. My emotional, mental, and spiritual state began to take their toll on my physical health and I was headed down fast. Living a lie and trying to keep everyone happy, despite your own brokenness can become impossible to do any longer.

Once at a women's conference I heard a Speaker say, "sometimes we live our lives as if we are holding a beach ball under water, it may pop up slightly from time to time, but you can keep it under the water, hidden away, pretty well. Then one day that ball becomes more buoyant and you get tired of fighting to keep it buried, fatigue sets in, and it gets to be too difficult. You get to a point you just can't hold it under any longer. That's when it begins to pop up and you try with all your might to push it back down. However, eventually it just keeps bobbing to the surface and slipping out of your control. it's an analogy for feelings you repress for years.

Next, a major life-altering event happened, September 11, 2001. My husband went almost immediately from reserve status with the Air Force to active duty status. Prior to the attacks on our country we had received orders to our new duty station, Michigan. We were apprehensive, but excited to see another part of the country. The events of September 11, 2001 put those orders on hold and my husband on night shift at the base in Massachusetts. We were relieved he wasn't going to have to deploy overseas and that our move would only be delayed a year.

Then, six months later came the orders. He was being deployed to Spain in support of the war effort. We were unsure for how long and if I would be able to care for our children in his absence, since I had been so ill for so long. So, we made the difficult decision to pack and store our household goods, move out of our rent house. The children and I would go down south while he was away. This way we would be closer to family in the event I got really sick I would have help caring for our children.

When we made this decision, we thought I would have several options of places to stay while there. Possibly my in-laws in Texas, my best friends in Louisiana, my sister in Mississippi, or as a last resort, my mother and stepdad. Well, can you guess which one I ended up having to stay with? My mother and stepdad. My sister-in-law and her family had moved in with my in-laws, so they only had room for us to come for short visits. My best friends' sister had moved in with them, because her husband was retiring from the military, they were moving to Louisiana and she wanted to start their children in school at the beginning of the year. No room there for us there either, only a weeklong visit when her sister was gone to visit family in another state. My sister, her husband deployed with the Navy on a sub, also in support of the war effort. She and her daughter were living in a tiny apartment, only room for a one week visit.

I knew staying with my mother and stepdad was going to be difficult, but I had no idea just how bad it would get. I told myself if we went and did things to be out of the house as much as possible it would be alright. If we could go visit everyone else and mainly stay away I could make it through the summer.

It worked well for about a month, then I started to unravel. I didn't know it at the time, but my children told me later. Every time my mother and stepdad fought, which was often, I would zone out, I shut down mentally. My children say they would call me and try to get my attention, but until they touched or shook me I was like a zombie. A coping mechanism learned long ago, as a means of self-protection from living in a traumatic household in childhood I suppose.

When we were away visiting friends and family I was myself, but as soon as we had to go back to my mothers and stepdads' house, zombie mom was back. I can't tell you how I felt, I don't think I felt much. I just went through every day in survival mode, much the same as I did when I was a child growing up in that home. I felt fine and functioned if they were at work or my children and I were out of the house, but otherwise I was just out of it, mentally.

As it happened, with the war winding down, after about a month into my husband's deployment they closed the base he was at and sent him back to Massachusetts to finish out his orders. Are you thinking awesome, now you can go back home and get away from your parent's house? One big problem, we had no house, all our household goods were in boxes, and being the middle of summer there was no space in any of the local campgrounds, for us to put our camper to live in. So, we decided the children and I would stay the rest of the summer in Texas, like we had originally planned. My husband would go back to Massachusetts and live in our camper while he finished out his orders, then we would transfer to our next duty station in Michigan.

We had friends that flipped houses for a living and he could put the camper in the driveway of the house they were flipping. He was working night shift again, so he helped work on the house during the day. Then one fateful night a couple of weeks later that all changed.

I had a major defining moment one Friday night at my mother and stepdads house. We still had a month and a half before we could go home and prepare for the move. My mother casually mentioned, "Your step-brother is coming by the house on his way from working the oils fields in south Texas. He is headed back to Louisiana." I immediately went on high alert, every synapse in my brain fired, I had this sense of dread, and overwhelming fear of being out of control. See two of my stepbrothers lived with us when I was nine and I was molested by them. The older one had been killed in a car accident many years earlier, but the other one was headed to the house.

My immediate thought was fear for the safety of my children. My girls were about the same age I was at the time of the abuse. I quickly called my husband, through tears I told him, "my stepbrother is coming here." He could tell by the sound of my voice something was very wrong, I told him, "I will not stay at this house if he is staying here. The children and I will go to a hotel. I will not let my children stay in the same house as him!" My husband was of course fine, saying, "you do what you need to protect yourself and our children." I fed the children an early dinner and tucked them safely in a back bedroom with their toys and a movie. I gave them strict instructions not to leave the room unless it was an emergency, if they needed me to open the door and call me. I then went to the living room, sat down at the table across from my mother and waited for his arrival.

While we were waiting my stepdad explained, "your step-brother is coming by because he is having trouble with his ATM card. He can't get any cash out for gas and money to go back to Louisiana." Then he proceeded to tell me why, "his ex-wife cleaned out his bank account when he got paid today, he gave her some signed checks to catch him up on his back-child support. She cashed a check for every bit of money he just got paid and there's no money in there for him to get out." My mother and stepdad knew this, but my stepbrother did not.

When my stepbrother arrived, he was obviously under the influence. He proceeded to tell my mother and stepdad, "my card isn't working, and I don't know why. I need to get gas and food money to get home, I don't know what I'm going to do." Instead of telling him why he couldn't get any cash out, my stepdad said, "we don't have an ATM card, but Elizabeth does, and she will ride down to the bank with you and help you get some cash."

I couldn't believe what I was hearing! I thought, I have three children in a bedroom in this house, they need a mother, and you want me to get in the car with a person who molested me as a child, who's under the influence, and go get money you know isn't there? I looked up at my mother, who, sat across the table from me. She looked up, made brief eye contact with me, then just looked down, she never uttered a word!

There I was, suddenly, the blinders on my eyes were finally gone, I was no longer a zombie, I was extremely mad and hurt. In that moment I thought, you really don't care about me, my safety, the safety of my children, once again I was devastated and broken hearted. However, it was the years of pent up anger that surfaced, I looked my stepdad in the face and said, "Like *HELL* I will!". I promptly got up, not making eye contact with any of them, went to the room where my children were and ask them one simple question, "do y'all want to go home?".

Their response socked me, they gave no verbal answer just got up and immediately started packing their belongings. No answer just a frantic pace to get their things together to leave this place. A wash of sadness came over me, realizing they didn't want to be there either. They wanted out as badly as I did.

I explained to them, "we will be living in the camper with no bathroom hook-ups, it's in the driveway of a house daddy's helping remodel. We will have to go inside the house to use the bathroom and bathe." To my surprise they were fine with that, they just wanted out of this house. I honestly had no idea they were so miserable there. Tears come to my eyes now thinking they felt that way at their grandparent's house. I had the most wonderful grandmother on the planet and I would have rather been with her, at her house than anywhere else on the planet when I was a child. My children did not feel that way in the least. It still breaks my heart.

While I was in the bedroom with my children my stepdad gave my stepbrother enough cash to get back to Louisiana. My stepbrother left. I don't know if they told him why he couldn't get cash out of the bank or not and I really don't care. I was just happy he was gone.

I did not have the strength or energy to confront my mother and stepdad, I simply told them we were ready to go home. We packed our things, loaded the car, and left bright and early the next morning.

We drove for days to get back to Massachusetts. I pushed though and kept myself together until safe again in my husband's arms. Then I fell apart emotionally. The depression was so dark and all consuming. It engulfed me like a dark storm I could no longer run from.

The next month is a blur of depression, anger, and night terrors. The phone calls and voice messages from my mother came with greater frequency. After a couple of weeks of restless sleep, with seemingly unending night terrors I finally drug myself out of bed. I felt I needed to explain to my mother what had happened. I sat down and after several drafts I finally finished a letter I thought explained how I was feeling and ask for what I needed most.

This is what I wrote:

August 28, 2002

Dear Mother,

I know you are wondering why you haven't heard from me. I did not return your call this weekend because I simply did not want to talk. I have been going through a lot emotionally and did not feel up to another superficial conversation.

Being back there this summer brought back a lot of very painful memories for me and I am trying to work out how I feel. There has always been a lot of strain on our relationship and I have never really had a relationship with my stepdad. I have always felt like a thorn in his side, the thing that always comes between the two of you. I expressed my feelings to you three years ago in hopes that something would change between us, but nothing has. I talk to you every weekend on the phone and see you once or twice a year but, there is still a wall between us.

My hope was that you would share the past with me and it would somehow release you from this terrible burden you have carried all these years. That the wall would begin to come down and we could have the mother-daughter relationship I have always wanted. But I am beginning to feel that will never happen. You seem to want to continue to pretend that none of it ever happened and everything is okay, but I am not okay.

I have always tried to do the right thing and I have always tried to make you happy and please you. All the while never quite measuring up and making myself miserable trying. I just can't do it anymore, I must do what is right and best for me now. I can't go on pretending. God is doing a mighty work in my life and healing my wounded spirit and I need time and space to heal.

I know I may never have answers to my questions about who my father is, until I get to Heaven. But I also know that right now I cannot continue the way I have been.

So, if you want to know how we are or what is going on, you can call my husband or the girls. If you want to see the kids, we will meet you somewhere. But for now, until things are resolved between us I need some time and space.

I love you and I thank God for you. I pray for you that you will let God in and let Him take this burden from you and heal you.

Love,
Elizabeth

Even though my letter was not venomous or hateful I hesitated to mail it. I knew my mother would not deal well with me wanting time and space. Being the very controlling person, she is. I guess the weekend phone calls made her feel like we had a good relationship or something, but they always felt strained and fake to me.

I stood outside the base in Massachusetts, looking at the mailbox's, frozen in fear to put the letter in. I knew once it was in there it was done, and I couldn't take it back. You may be asking, after all of this why would you not want to send the letter and have this be over? Well, I think because that relationship was all I knew and without it I didn't know what life would be like. I knew enough to know for me to speak up would change everything and the fear of the unknown is very real.

I suppose as a child of a dysfunctional family a messed-up relationship somehow seems better than no relationship at all. When you've lived with dysfunction for so long, you have no idea what life is like without it. Will it be better? Could it be worse? You just don't know and not knowing is terrifying.

I didn't have long to wait to find out how the relationship would change. My children were sitting in the car waiting for me to put the letter in the mailbox. They watched as I stood there frozen, unable to pull the door open and drop the letter in. That's when my headstrong, middle daughter got out of the car, pulled the envelope from my fear frozen fingers and dropped it in the box. It was done. There was no getting it back, it was on its way to Texas and all there was to do now was wait. Not that there was anything in that letter that should cause a problem in a normal relationship, but this was not normal and never had been.

Time and space, that is the main thing I ask for, but I knew my mother couldn't give it to me. Just as I had expected a couple of weeks later my sister called. She asks, "What is going on with you and mom? Every time I talk to her all she does is cry. She said when you left there, you left a letter saying you never wanted to see her again." Well, I must admit I wasn't surprised, the manipulation had begun.

Fortunately, I had made a photo copy of the letter I sent my mother. I told my sister, "I will make a copy of the letter and sent it to you, so you know exactly what I said and when I sent it." I knew enough, from living this way my entire life, that my words would be twisted and changed if I didn't have proof of what the letter said. I mailed my sister a copy of the letter the next day.

CHAPTER 4

My Attempt to Break Free
Should You Dare to Dream
that Unbrokenness is Even
Possible?

*The most difficult thing is the decision to act, the rest
is merely tenacity.—Amelia Earhart*

One month later we moved to Michigan. We had a contract to purchase a home and while we were waiting to close on our new house the military put us in temporary housing for two months. It was one of the most difficult times of my life. Trying to manage the all-consuming depression, homeschool our children, maintain normalcy, all the while I felt like I was coming completely unraveled.

The hurt and pain became more difficult to hide. The cracks in my soul began to break apart and what they unearthed was a whole lot of anger. The anger was like the hot magma in a volcano that had sat dormant for years, it began to spew out in spurts of anger and rage. Unfortunately, where does lava hit when it erupts? All over the things closest to it. For me that was my husband and children. They began to see little spurts of magma, then as time went on and the cracks opened wider there came multiple explosions of red-hot lava. It flew at everyone in my path, spraying, burning, and hurting them in ways I never intended.

Then the first email came. My mother had apparently gotten herself together enough to email my children. She wrote to them telling them I had sent a letter saying I didn't ever want to see her again, but if their dad would meet her and my stepdad half way between Texas and Michigan she would take them shopping and out to eat. *Lies, All lies.* However, what she did not realize was my husband and children knew everything. I had told my girls years earlier that my stepdad was not my biological father, I had not, however, told my son. I felt he was too young at five to understand. They had read the letter I sent her before I'd ever mailed it. The one asking for time and space to sort out my feelings. Every member of my family approved it before it was mailed. So, she had no way of getting away with the lies.

Our daughters replied to her email, explaining they knew everything and had read the letter before it was sent. They told her they knew I had said she could contact them anytime and that my husband would bring them to meet her. She then began emailing them on a regular basis. Once we moved into our house in late November, the girls sent her the home phone number, so she could call them. The calls began that next weekend and came right on schedule every Sunday afternoon. I would look at the caller ID, see that it was her and tell the children the phone was for them.

The conversation, if that's what you want to call it, lasted an average of five minutes, with the phone being passed between our three children and my mother saying, "I don't have anything to talk about, you talk". After a few weeks of this my children were tired of playing this game and didn't want to answer the phone anymore, I told them if they didn't want to talk on the phone they didn't have to, so they stopped answering. That's when my stepdad began to call and leave hateful messages on the voicemail. He said, "You need to straighten up and let those children to talk to your mother." This was nothing new and I just ignored it, but my middle daughter wasn't having any of it.

She was tired of the games, the hateful voice messages, and the mistreatment of me. She sat down and wrote my mother an email. She was extraordinarily mature for the ripe old age of fourteen and penned what I believed was a thoughtful, well-written explanation of why they didn't want to talk. However, my mother and stepdad did not see it that way. My mother wrote an extremely venomous email back and so it began.

My husband had once again been deployed overseas with the military in February after we moved to Michigan. He was away for a month this time and I was once again left to keep everything together on the home front. I kept him informed with emails and short phone conversations about the situation. However, the email from my mother to our daughter was the last straw for him. He had let me handle the situation up until then, but he was not about to stand by and let anyone talk to his daughter that way.

I sat down and wrote my mother an email telling her that the way she spoke to our daughter was completely unacceptable, and she would not speak to my children that way. I also forwarded all the emails to my husband overseas. After reading the entirety of the communication that went back and forth, my calm, easygoing husband had enough.

He and I had made an agreement when we got married that any issues we had with our own families would be handled by us and the spouse would not get involved unless asked to. However, this time it was his child she was lashing out at and that crossed the line for him. He sent her an email telling her he would not tolerate her speaking out of anger to any of his children. The problems between her and I were between us, but do not contact the children again. If they want to contact her, they have the phone number and address and they will contact her.

He called me to discuss the situation. As I stood looking out the glass doors of our new home, snow blowing in drifts all around the house. The scene I was looking at out my door was as cold and desolate as I was feeling. Talking to my husband on the phone, I said as tears streamed down my face, "I just want to disappear". My poor husband, helpless across the world thought I meant suicide. *No!* Nothing was further from the truth. I just wanted to escape, find a small hole and crawl into it, tend the deep, ever bigger gaping open cracks in my soul, and try to find my way out of this pit of despair. That was it, the dominos of my sanity began to fall in rapid succession.

I sent one more letter hoping it might make my point and explain my feelings.

February 7, 2003

Dear Mom and stepdad,

Well it seems it is time for me to get involved. I have thought and prayed a lot about how this will go and no matter what I do or say it never turns out the way I hoped it would. You and I came to a crossroads three years ago, when I could no longer live the lies that have plagued me all my life and you cannot face the truth. I went back to playing along with your game of pretend and lies, but I'm at a point in my life where I will no longer accept that as a way of life. I wrote you a letter last August, because when I got back from down there I was in such a state of depression that I could not function. Being back in your home with all the fighting and arguing brought back so many horrible memories for me, that you can't even imagine. It is not that I don't want to talk to you anymore, it's just that I don't want to play pretend everything is fine and that we have a mother/daughter relationship and most of all I don't want to be lied to anymore!

I will be happy to talk with you, when you are ready to tell me the truth. I cannot continue to have a superficial relationship like we have had. I must find peace and healing for myself. I am seeing a counselor to help me work through all of this and you should too.

As I have told you, I know I may not have the answers to my question of who my father is this side of Heaven, but that doesn't mean I will give up trying to find out. I will do whatever it takes to unravel the lies, find the truth, and get the answers I so desperately need. You hold the keys, but you do not hold all the keys and I will seek out anyone who can shed light on the situation and tell me the truth. If you don't want me to do this you have the power to stop me, by telling me the truth. It's your call the truth or nothing. I hope you choose to tell me the truth.

Elizabeth

I was not only fighting my mother and stepdad, but also this dark monster of depression that was rapidly engulfing me. I was feeling exhausted and sad, but I attempted to push that beach ball under the water again and power through. I just wanted to run and hide from the awful experiences of the last ten months.

Things continued to get worse for me, the beach ball now floating on top of the water, no possibility of getting it back under the water again, not even a little bit. I became very ill within days of sending that letter, with severe bronchitis and constant asthma attacks, so bad I had to call the military base for someone to take me to the doctor and take my daughters to the grocery store. I couldn't function, I spent the next few weeks on the couch as sick as I can ever remember being, up until then. Pumped full of antibiotics and steroids just trying to breathe and survive. Finally, at the end of his deployment my husband came home, and I tried so hard to get our life back to normal.

Letters began to come from my mother and stepdad with regularity, and none answering my questions. Some of the things they said were so hurtful and a lot of it didn't even make sense. My mother said in one of the letters that my biological father gave her a fake name. That my grandmother told her someone called once but she didn't take a message.

She said she was sorry I was so sick and that our oldest daughter had developed asthma as well, but doctors treat people all the time with less family history than I had.

My uncle sent a letter also. His letter was one of the most hurtful of all. I had not seen or talked to them for four or five years, so I was surprised to get a letter from him, but after reading it I was more hurt than before. He said, he could understand me wanting to know about my dad, and to know about my heritage, but some things are impossible. What you are asking your mother for is impossible for her.

He said he was there through it all, and he saw the affects my birth had on my mother. He saw her cry, depressed, and hurt. He told me he met my biological father several times. That he came to their house to see my mother. He said one Sunday afternoon. Apparently, my biological father even came by once and my uncle was the only one home. They spent the biggest part of the day together. He was very well dressed, very clean-cut man, and drove a nice car. As a matter of fact, he said he really liked him and thought he was very good for my mother. So, what is the problem then, just tell me his name.

He said that in both mine and my husband's letters, we said we were praying for my mother, and he didn't understand why, because it appears to him that she has already been tried, judged, and crucified by both of us. He said please, for my sake, don't add me to your prayers, for Christ said by what measure we judge, we will be judged. If this holds true, then I am afraid the day will come in your life that the cold, harsh, words of hatred will return to you. James 3:8 says, "The tongue can no man tame, it is unruly evil, full of deadly poison. "Therefore, if your letters come from your heart, then Christ is not there, and you are living a lie yourself, and blaming your mother.

Those words cut so deep that I thought for sure I would go under and never come back up. Every letter that came was another knife to my heart, until I just couldn't take it anymore. I was becoming completely unwound emotionally, not able to function. The volcano that had begun to spew lava in small spurts suddenly erupted, I was spewing hot lava on everyone in my vicinity. I was out of control, it was like an out-of-body experience, watching myself act like an insane person and not knowing how to make it stop.

Then the last straw, a certified letter from my mother. Essentially, she said she couldn't believe I would act this way. I'd tell lies about the things that happened to me. I would turn her grandchildren against her. But she would leave us alone. Finally, that's all I wanted, to be left alone for a while, so I could sort out my feelings.

I sent one last letter:

May 9, 2003

Mom and stepdad,

I am writing one last letter in hopes of getting you to understand how all of this has affected me. I am in counseling and under a doctor's care trying to sort out everything that I have been through and the reasons I am unable to help you understand how traumatic it's been for me.

I am asking you one last time, please tell me who my father is. I desperately need to know the family's health history, especially their mental health history. I'm sorry but I do not believe he gave you a fake name. I believe that you just don't want me to know who he is or to have any kind of relationship with him. Weather out of pure selfishness or some self-serving noble act you believe you are doing to protect me. It's not protecting me, it's hurting me not knowing the truth and not being able to provide my caregivers with complete health history information.

I am begging you, please share whatever information you can remember with me. My husband will be monitoring the mail and phone if you have a change of heart and wish to tell me what I so desperately need to know.

Elizabeth

That was it the last communication. You would think it would bring sweet relief, but I was so hurt, angry, and guilty I could no longer contain my emotions.

The lava spewed in every direction all over my children and husband. I would take long walks and spew at God. Now, you may be shocked by that, I figured God is a big God and quite capable of handling my angry outburst. I told him I was so mad, in a rage to be exact. I ask questions like why you would put me in that family and I cried until there were no tears left.

PART 3

HEALING –
The Path

CHAPTER 5

The Path to Healing Physically

Are you sick and tired of being sick and tired?

Healing is an art. It takes time, it takes practice,
it takes love.—unknown

The years of stress and feelings of being unworthy, unloved, unwanted, and a burden had left me very physically ill. I could not get well no matter what I did. I learned growing up on the family farm by my grandmothers' side about natural methods of healing and when we lived in northern Florida, I met a couple of homeschooling moms that believed in natural healing. In our short time in Florida I learned a lot from my friends and by the time the illnesses began to overwhelm me, I was already considering how to heal naturally.

Having a holistic view, I believe God created us to be a four-part person, physical, emotional, mental, and spiritual. I knew I needed balance in all four areas of my life, but I was so sick I had no idea where to start. I began doing a lot of research online, trying to put the pieces of this complicated puzzle together.

My asthma was completely out of control. After seeing an allergist and getting an allergy testing on my back, my body reacted by swelling into huge welts everywhere the test touched. I spent days after the testing laying on my stomach with ice packs on the red, swollen, knots on my back. The allergist of course, said this meant I was allergic to everything they tested for. How could I be allergic to everything they tested for? How in the world could I be allergic to every plant, tree, animal, and everything else on the planet? I wasn't.

My body was so overwhelmed, toxic, stressed, and flooded with adrenaline that absolutely every stimulus sent my immune system into overdrive. I reacted to foods, water, scents, and cold air. No matter what it was my body would overreact to it. A scent from an object as simple as a flower would cause an asthma attack. I could eat food I had enjoyed my entire life, and now my face would turn bright red and swell. I would break out in hives on my entire body, with no idea what was causing it. I began keeping a food and symptom diary, and I could find no rhyme or reason for these symptoms.

I began researching online for reasons I might be having these overreactions. That's when I found an online college that offered degrees in Natural Health. I was ecstatic! I could take college courses and not worry about us transferring with my husband's military career and changing colleges. They accepted my credits from the other colleges I had attended and offered some testing for specific courses, by the time I was finished with the enrollment process I only had a year and a half of classes to take to complete my Bachelors' in Holistic Nutrition.

They offered additional training at conferences once a year. You go to an intensive four-day event and the classes you take apply towards your degree. I attended the conference my first year as a student and met a chiropractor who worked with patients with Chronic Fatigue Syndrome and Fibromyalgia. As I sat listening to his presentation it became abundantly clear to me, this must be what I was experiencing. I bought his book, *Treating and Beating Chronic Fatigue and Fibromyalgia*, and began consuming every word on the flight home.

I fit the profile for Chronic Fatigue more than Fibromyalgia simply because of the extreme exhaustion I was experiencing, no matter how much I slept. In addition, I did not have the chronic widespread pain of Fibromyalgia. I was so exhausted I would fall asleep sitting at the dining room table, helping my son with his schoolwork. I felt like I could sleep twenty hours a day and still not feel rested. I also had an extremely weakened immune system, although it had always been compromised. For as long as I could remember, I was either sick, on medication, or coming down with something. When I had my tonsils taken out at age seventeen, the doctors literally had to scrape the sides of my throat. My tonsils had been infected so many times they had grown into the walls of my throat.

Now that I knew what to call this thing that had caused my body to be so sick and exhausted, I could develop a path toward healing. First, the thirty plus years of stress had made my body toxic, so I desperately needed to detox my body and begin to replace the deficient nutrients.

I began to apply the principles I was learning in my classes, and what I learned from the lecture and book, *Treating and Beating Chronic Fatigue and Fibromyalgia* written by Dr. Rodger H. Murphree, to my life. I started to see physical healing begin ever so slowly. I began by addressing the stress in my life. Stress, in my opinion, is the number one cause of illness and death in western society. We go through life stressed to the max and ignore the signals our bodies are sending us. Signals such as I need extra sleep, or we recognize the signals, but don't know what to do about them. Let's examine what that stress looks like and what I did to begin healing my body physically.

Stress, according to The Cleveland Clinic, is the body's reaction to any change that requires an adjustment or response. The body reacts to these changes with physical, mental, and emotional responses. Stress is a normal part of life. You can experience stress from your environment, your body, and your thoughts. Even positive life changes such as a promotion, a mortgage, or the birth of a child produce stress. (8)

Your body and mind can't tell the difference in a serious threat, like being robbed or events that are not life threatening like dieting. Remember the Adverse Childhood Experiences Study, "discovered when inflammatory stress hormones flood a child's body and brain, they alter the genes that oversee our stress reactivity, re-setting the stress response to "high" for life.

This increases the risk of inflammation, because our fight, flight or freeze response is rewired." (5)

Increased stress manifests in the body in multiple ways:

1. Increased levels of stress hormones, like cortisol

2. Blood sugar rises

3. Altered appetite

4. Altered digestion (by changing the gut environment)

5. Affecting how thyroid glands and hormones work

Some symptoms of chronic stress:

1. Tension headaches

2. Fatigue

3. Raised blood pressure

4. Heart disease

5. Obesity

When short spikes in cortisol and adrenaline happen repeatedly throughout the day, they cause wear and tear on the body and speed up the aging process. So, imagine what continued daily stress for years does to your body. These symptoms just multiply and the effect is much greater. (9)

I began by focusing on my diet to detoxify my body. We are bombarded by toxins in every part of modern life, our air, water, food, and just about everything we encounter puts a toxic load on our bodies. This isn't usually a problem for people with a healthy immune system, but for those of us who have a compromised immune system, we become like the canary in the coal mine. Coal miners used to take canaries down in the coal mines with them as a way of alerting them if the toxic gasses were too high. The canaries were more sensitive to the toxic fumes and if they died the coal miners knew to get out because the levels of toxins were too high, and they would soon succumb to the same fate as the canaries. (10) Perhaps those of us with chronic illness are the new canaries in the coal mines, alerting others of the toxicity in our environment.

To lessen the toxic load on our body, we need to begin by reducing the load of toxins we take in through our food, water, and medication. I believe there are benefits to all types of medical treatments and we need to adopt an integrated approach to healing. Western medicine is excellent, but I believe we need a balance between the best of western medicine and alternative therapies. Medicine is not an all or nothing proposition, we can take the best of many different therapies and come to a balanced way to heal ourselves. One thing I did to begin this process was to search out holistic practitioners online and try different things, until I found what worked for me.

I used my education and the book *Treating and Beating Chronic Fatigue Syndrome and Fibromyalgia* by: Dr. Rodger H. Murphee, to make a holistic healing plan and began to implement it by doing the following:

1. Eating a whole, organic food diet

2. Getting good quality sleep

3. Regular Chiropractic Care

4. Taking Hot Mineral Baths

5. Regular Massage Therapy

6. Exercise and fresh air daily

7. Practicing Yoga or Tia Chi

8. Taking good high-quality Vitamins, Minerals, and Herbal Supplements

Eat a Whole Food, Organic Diet

Eating a whole organic food diet is one of the best things you can do to help your body begin to detoxify and heal. We didn't have much money as a military family of five, but I knew it was vitally important that I get foods that didn't add more toxins from pesticides and other chemicals to my body. I found a local Amish market where I could buy organic chicken, eggs, butter, fruits and vegetables. I was pleasantly surprised to find that shopping there was not costing me any extra money, just a twenty-minute drive to the market. I also joined a local farmers' co-op that delivered a box of organic fresh fruits and vegetables to specific locations in town once a week for pick-up.

Then I either purchased other organic foods at the regular grocery store or drove to Whole Foods Store once a month. I cut out all junk food, prepackaged foods and started eating clean at least eighty percent of the time. I say eighty percent because nothing in life is all or nothing, and if I didn't give myself some wiggle room to occasionally have a treat I would have caused myself more stress.

Get Good Quality Sleep

Getting good quality sleep is very high on the list for healing when it comes to any illness, especially chronic illness. "During sleep, your body is working to support healthy brain function and maintain your physical health." (7) I set up a sleep schedule as best as I could, making sure to go to bed at the same time every night and get up at the same time every morning, but it wasn't helping with my exhaustion. Then I was diagnosed with Sleep Apnea and prescribed a CPAP machine. Before I was diagnosed, I was getting quite mad at our cat because he never slept with us, but he would wait until I fell asleep and then sleep on my pillow. Several times a night he would reach over and put one claw in my forehead just enough to wake me. This made me quite mad, but after the Sleep Apnea diagnoses I realized I must have stopped breathing and he was simply waking me up, to restart my breathing. If you have pets, pay attention to their behavior. They may be more aware of your health than you are and are simply alerting you to issues or protecting you.

Chiropractic Care

Getting regular chiropractic care was an important part of my healing.

I read in *Treating and Beating Chronic Fatigue and Fibromyalgia* how important body alignment is. I had never seen a chiropractor, so I ask people I knew for a referral. The chiropractor I was referred to was excellent and this simple step made a really big difference, especially in my asthma and Sleep Apnea. He wanted me to be comfortable and at ease. The adjustment to your spine can be done manually by the doctor or with a small tool called an activator. Chiropractors apply gentle pressure to your spine to help your vertebra go back into proper alignment, so that your spinal column and nerves function properly. I started going two times a week, then once a week, and finally, once a month as I improved over the course of two years.

I had no idea what to expect from chiropractic care. I was pleasantly surprised that the Chiropractor was easygoing and gentle in nature, which set me at ease. Finding a practitioner who will listen is vitally important. Find a practitioner that listens to you and that you feel comfortable with. If you begin seeing any practitioner and you don't feel comfortable and at ease, find someone else.

You are the customer, something practitioners need to understand. You are free to go to someone else if you're not satisfied with the service they are providing. And if need be, you have the power to fire any service provider and hire a team player who supports you in your efforts to heal naturally. You want doctors and caregivers who understand that you are trying to heal your body and not ones that cause you more stress.

Hot Mineral Baths

Mineral baths are wonderfully relaxing; however, they are also a great way to help the mind and body heal. I was fortunate that we lived in Michigan at the time, home of the Mt. Clemens Springs. Mineral hot springs provide benefits for our health and healing, but since western medicine has become more dominant in American society, people have forgotten the benefits of healing waters. An individual now owns the Mt. Clemens Baths. He harvests the minerals from the springs and removes the smelly sulfur. You can now go to Mt. Clemens Medical Center, they have a large modern spa where you can soak in the hot mineral water for twenty minutes and get a one-hour healing massage. I tried to make sure I did this at least once a month to help my body heal and detoxify.

Hot Springs, Arkansas also has a hotel, The Arlington Resort Hotel and Spa, where you can go and enjoy soaking in the old bathhouse and be pampered for a few hours or an entire day. If you are not close to any of these types of businesses, you can purchase the minerals and enjoy a hot mineral bath at home. You can also make your own mineral bath mixture or bath bombs and soak in those. Epsom Salt is an amazing mineral soak and very relaxing and detoxing for the body. Epsom Salt contains magnesium, which along with the hot water, relaxes the muscles and is especially good before bed with a few drops of lavender essential oil to help you relax and get a good night's sleep.

Massage Therapy

Getting massage therapy was one of the best things for my body. Massage therapy is not only relaxing, but also helps remove toxins from the body as has been recognized for thousands of years. The Romans and Greeks used it as a regular healing treatment. Western Society needs to return to therapies with thousands of years of proof backing them up. (11)

Find a massage therapist that works for you, listens to you, and knows multiple massage techniques, so you receive the best possible outcome. Visiting several massage therapists may be necessary to find the right one. During my healing I tried different types of massage therapy to find what my body needed and went at least once a month. Remember this is a prescription for healing, not an indulgence. Massage therapy is a vital part of detoxifying and healing your body.

Fresh Air and Exercise

Our bodies need exercise and fresh air to aid in detoxification and healing. Every cell in our body requires oxygenation and we need to help our bodies wash its cells in healing oxygen. The best way to do this is a gentle morning and/or evening walk. The exercise stretches, relaxes, and heals, while bathing the cells in fresh air. Now I know what you're saying, "but Elizabeth, I'm so tired and sore. I don't have the energy to exercise. If I exercise, I'm just more sore and more exhausted." I know. I've been there. Start with just two to three minutes and build up from there. You will be more tired and sore at first, but after a week or so you'll start to notice your walk makes you feel better. Don't power walk or try to get your heart rate up. That will come in time. Right now, you are focusing on healing, and you need to be gentle and loving with yourself. No harsh anything.

Yoga or Tia Chi

Yoga and Tia Chi combine meditation, slow movements, deep breathing and relaxation. They have both been found to be extremely helpful for many symptoms of Chronic Illness. If you are a beginner and can go to classes to learn from a certified teacher, that is best. Then you can practice at home to help control your symptoms. You can purchase relaxation yoga DVDs and do the gentle poses and stretches to help relax your muscles. Again, you are flooding your body with oxygen and helping your muscles relax and return to their non-constricted state, which is healing and detoxifying for your body. (12)

Vitamins, Minerals, and Herbal Supplements

Use Vitamins, Herbs and Supplements to cleanse and nourish the body.

My body needed help to release the toxins that had built up from years of brokenness and oxidative stress. Oxidation causes the body to accelerate the aging process and the more oxidative stress you have the faster the aging process and onset of chronic illness. This stress causes the body to become toxic and unable to absorb the nutrients we need to heal. (9) The level of illness I was experiencing was due to my body's inability to remove toxins and absorb enough nutrients to heal. Based on the suggestions from *Treating and Beating Fibromyalgia and Chronic Fatigue*, I started on high doses of vitamins and mineral supplement to restore and replace what I was deficient in. When you're under long-term stress and your body is toxic you not only need to be sure you're getting the nutrients you need daily, but also replace what is deficient. High quality, readily absorbable vitamin and mineral supplements will best serve this purpose.

These are some healing techniques and supplements I used to heal my broken body and restore my health. You should always get guidance from a trained natural health practitioner. You should never undertake a program of healing on your own, without the guidance of an educated practitioner. You need help determining what your body needs and guidance on the amounts and types of supplements to take. Supplements are medication and you would never just grab a prescription from someone's medicine cabinet and start taking it without advice from your doctor or pharmacist, the same is true for supplements.

Healing does not happen overnight, but with patience and commitment, healing will come, and you will begin to see improvements. The absolute best thing you can do for your body, while it's in crisis mode, is to be loving and gentle with it. Every ache, pain, and other symptom is your body crying out to you, letting you know something is wrong. Your job is to listen and learn what your body needs. Loving your body is the first step to healing the brokenness and regaining your life.

CHAPTER 6

My Path to Healing Mentally

Are you trapped in a mental prison?

"A person whose mind is quite and satisfied in God, is in the pathway to health."—Ellen G. White

I thought the path to mental healing was going to be the most difficult area of healing. Now, I don't think it was, but replacing the negative messages I replayed in my mind was certainly difficult. Healing the mind takes time, patience, and hard work. I and others like me who have suffered in a dysfunctional and abusive home, have much work to do. Years of destructive messages play like a song on repeat in our heads, always telling us that we are not, "good enough, pretty enough, smart enough, or everything is our fault and life would be better without us." That was at least true for me.

I don't know if in every case the messages were meant to tear me down or if they were all said out loud, but those are just a few of the things I felt and heard. As an adult who has been through many years of counseling, I really don't believe it was my family's intention to tear me down, but they did whether intentional or not. Hurting people simply hurt people. They had issues carried over from their lives, which they projected on me.

Whatever the case, that pain and those scars cut deep and took time to heal. Believe me; we cannot rush through healing our minds. I know because I tried to just put my head down and power through it, but it took time and effort on my part. As with physical healing, we need a guide to walk the path with us. For me that was Kathy, my counselor and confidante.

Whether the person you choose is a friend, family member, coach, or professional counselor, you need someone to help you sort out the mental pain, heal the scars, and replace the negative thoughts with positive ones.

I was so broken mentally, I find it hard even now to put the pain into words. Our mind is the master controller of the rest of who we are, and when it is so broken, the rest of our being cannot function and be well. I so badly wanted that part of my journey to be over and behind me. After all, who really wants to walk back through all that crap? I would have much preferred to skip over it and move on to something else, but, we cannot allow any brokenness to remain unhealed if you want complete healing and wellness.

The Bible says, "But the tongue can no man tame; it is an unruly evil, full of deadly poison." (James 3:8 KJV) I know that is true, however, your thoughts are hard to overcome and control, as well. This is especially true when all you have heard your entire life is negative. Now, is that all that was said to me? Probably not. But it is what I heard, especially from my mother and stepdad. My grandmother gave me positive messages and affirmation and my teachers did as well. I heard those, but for some reason all I heard from my mother and stepdad was negative. Thinking back now, I must work hard to remember any positive messages from them. I'm sure there were some. I was, however, programmed to hear the negative. It was habit or easier to hear only the negative because that's what I believed.

For me the road to healing my thinking was to walk through each of those negative thoughts and learn to replace them with the truth. Kathy taught me that when one of those negative thoughts came into my head, and that was often. I should say "*Stop!*" Then replace it with the truth, the truth being the Word of God.

The Word of God is powerful, and it is the Truth. It is the perfect place to go to replace the bad with good. Believing what the Word of God said was hard at first because I believed the lies for so long. I had to practice recognizing the negative messages. I was so indoctrinated with the lies that I believed they were true, even though I had evidence that proved otherwise.

A good example of this is the negative message, "you're an idiot". I knew that could not be true. After all, I was now in my mid-thirties, happily married with three great children. I had opened and run multiple businesses with excellence, and I was a straight A student in both high school and college. I received scholarships for my excellence in academics, so I could not possibly be an idiot. However, I had heard that repeated time and time again for as long as I can remember. Not believing it was true was hard, even though all evidence said otherwise.

Our enemy, Satan, and our mind use this trick on us. These messages could not possibly be true, but since my stepdad favorite thing to call you was an idiot, it's what I believed from a very young age. The worst part is those negative messages run on a loop in our heads. Not only is that what we were told and believe, but now we repeat it to ourselves every hour of every day. Believing the positive is very difficult, because we have believed the lies for so long or worse yet, told ourselves the lie.

My mother would also use my physical illnesses, in childhood, like a weapon against me. Like I said in chapter one, I was physically ill my entire life. I caught every virus that went around my home and school. I would make my just-about-monthly visit to the doctor for antibiotics and steroids, so my mother could take me back to daycare and return to work as soon as possible. I remember hearing, "your sick again", or "we can't afford this". Even after I was grown and married, my mother would comment, "Well, you know we are a lot better off financially now that you're married because your medical bills kept us broke!". Hearing those comments made me feel guilty and ashamed for being sick, even though the sickness was out of my control. I felt like my family had to go without due to my very expensive medical bills. To this day, if I get sick, I feel guilty. As if I can control being sick. Some of those messages are incredibly hard to overcome.

My mother's control and negativity also affected my marriage for years. My husband is a very loving, caring, compassionate, and positive person. Every day he told me I was wonderful, special, smart, and pretty. I wanted desperately to believe him, but the tapes in my head just would not relent. He would complement me, but the tape would say the opposite. Since I was programmed to believe the tapes, I would blow off every complement he made. It's very confusing and hard for someone who has not been there to understand. He tried to understand, but he couldn't. He always felt hurt, because I just could not believe what he was telling me, and he thought that meant I did not believe him. The negative messages in my head were too loud for his voice to get through. The negative messages are easier to believe, especially when you've been trained to hear them above everything else.

After many years of hard, intentional work I have overcome most of the negative messages. I have managed to erase most of those tapes and record truth over the lies, but not all. I start my day by reading Scripture, Kathy taught me to replace the lies with the truth, I had to completely saturate my mind and spirit with the Word of God. When a specific scripture speaks to me, I write it on an index card. I keep a recipe box to file them in with category cards that say, faith, encouragement, child of God, and hope, written on them. Often, I write two or three cards with the same scripture on them and place one in my box, one in my purse, and one on the bathroom mirror or window sill in front of the kitchen sink. Every time I see it, I read it multiple times every day. As negative messages began to play, I have learned to exclaim, "*NO!* That is not the truth." and read the scripture out loud and repeat it. Doing this helps me erase the lies and record the truth in my brain.

In addition, I also changed what and who I allow to influence my thoughts. I listen to only positive, uplifting music. No sad songs. I only watch positive shows and movies. No more sad tear jerkers, unless I just need a good cry. And don't we all need that from time to time? I absolutely try to surround myself with positive people, I refuse to let others drag me back into the pit of despair. Now that doesn't mean I won't be friends with someone going through a tough time, but I try to help them get out of that place. If that person isn't willing to try and do the work, I must walk away. I won't go back to that place of negativity ever again, nor will I let another person pull me in.

I believe the most important choice I made to heal my mind was when I separated from my family. Deciding to walk away from abusive people, no matter who they are, is incredibly hard. Ending all communication with my family broke my heart, but it had to be done for my sanity and healing. I simply could not stay in a relationship with people who were mistreating me and get healthy, it was not possible. Everything I did to heal, they tore down. I kept rebuilding from the rubble, just to have it all torn down again. Breaking away was the hardest thing I have ever done, but the past fifteen years since I did, has given me the ability to rebuild myself physically, mentally, emotionally, and spiritually; something I could not have done if I let them remain in my life and continue to tear down the hard work I had accomplished.

Healing mentally takes hard work, commitment, and dare I say courage. It's hard and it is work. However, it can be done, I'm living proof of that. There will be days when it seems an impossible mountain to climb, but there will be good days too. You must keep pushing through until the good days outnumber the bad. As you continue pushing through, eventually the good days will outweigh the bad ones. And I'm always here if you need help climbing the mountains or company walking through the valleys. It's a much easier journey when you have a guide and some company, especially someone who has walked the path before and knows the way.

CHAPTER 7

My Path to Healing Emotionally

How high are your walls?

What we achieve inwardly will change outer reality.
—Plutarch

The dictionary defines emotions this way, "a natural instinctive state of mind deriving from one's circumstances, mood, or relationships with others." (13)

Robert Plutchik was professor emeritus at the Albert Einstein College of Medicine and adjunct professor at the University of South Florida. His theory says that the eight basic emotions are:

* Fear → feeling of being afraid

* Anger → feeling angry. A stronger word for anger is rage

* Sadness → feeling sad. Other words are sorrow, grief (a stronger feeling, for example when someone has died)

* Joy → feeling happy. Other words are happiness, gladness

* Disgust → feeling something is wrong or nasty

* Surprise → being unprepared for something

* Trust → a positive emotion; admiration is stronger; acceptance is weaker.

* Anticipation → in the sense of looking forward positively to something which is going to happen. Expectation is more neutral. (14)

Emotions play an important role in how we think and behave. The emotions we feel can compel us to act and influence the decisions we make, both large and small. Emotions can be a great help to us, but they can also do us great harm if we let them control us. Being completely broken emotionally, I cannot even explain how far out of sync my emotions were compared to someone who can process their emotions in a healthy way.

I was experiencing every negative emotion known to man. I was angry, sad, disappointed, enraged, devastated, and depressed. It was near impossible for me to experience joy and trust.

Lack of trust was nothing new for me. I had never really trusted anyone, so not trusting was normal for me. I had at this point, been married to the most wonderful, kind, loving, faithful husband for more than twenty years and I still didn't trust him. I feel terrible about that now, but life had taught me very well, no one can be trusted. He had never given me any reason to distrust him, but when a person has spent an entire lifetime trusting only herself, trusting anyone else is nigh impossible.

The only joy I found during this time was my children. Their little faces, pure hearts, and abundant laughter filled my heart with joy but only fleetingly. Then the depression and anger pulled me back in the pit. I just could not understand why this kept happening when I had confronted all my experiences. I could not understand why my family had turned on me like a pack of bloodthirsty wolves. The memories of what they said and did to me always came rushing back to my mind and stole any glimpses of joy I found.

Weeks after the last letter from my family I was still in bed or a rocking chair in my room. I was like a zombie staring at the wall, sleeping, or at other times a volcano trying to function and spewing lava at any given moment or for no reason. I had tried so hard to make my family understand how I felt, having them all turn on me like they did left my heart completely shattered.

The dark, deep hole of depression had completely engulfed me now.

I knew I needed help, as I slipped into the abyss of hopelessness. It wasn't my first time to visit that dark place, but I knew it was worse and I was in danger of going so deep in that I may never find my way out. The letters, emails, and phone calls from my family had finally stopped. But, I knew this time I couldn't pull myself back out without help.

The reason my entire family turned on me was beginning to become clear to me now. I came to the realization that I must be the child of narcissistic parents. "A narcissistic parent is defined as someone who lives through, is possessive of, and/or engages in marginalizing competition with the offspring. Typically, the narcissistic parent perceives the independence of a child (including adult children) as a threat and coerces the offspring to exist in the parent's shadow, with unreasonable expectations. In a narcissistic parenting relationship, the child is rarely loved just for being herself or himself. (15)

Most parents exhibit a few of the following traits from time to time. However, a narcissistic parent tends to dwell habitually in several of the following but remain largely unaware of (or unconcerned with) how these behaviors affect their child. (16)

Narcissistic Parents display some of all the following:

Uses/Lives Through One's Child
Marginalization of the Child
Grandiosity & Superiority

Superficial Image
Manipulation
Inflexible and Touchy
Lack of Empathy
Dependency/Codependency
Jealousy & Possessiveness
Neglect

My mother and stepdad exhibited many of these. I often wonder what happened to them. What made them this way? I guess I will never know the answer, but whatever it was I do know how it affected me and I still fight the affects every day.

Often, narcissistic people use a technique called gaslighting to control you.

After every letter, email, and phone call I began to question myself, thinking if my entire family believed I was attacking my mother and being unfair to her, then maybe I was the crazy one. The thing is, a narcissist manipulates everyone in their life and they get so good at it that others don't even realize they are being manipulated. They believe whatever the narcissist tells them, even if they see the words with their own eyes. The narcissistic twist the context and makes the target, in this situation me, seem like the crazy one. They convince others you are out to get them, ungrateful, and being manipulated by other people in your life.

I feel like my mother and stepdad had done this for years, blaming my husband for turning me against them when I decided to marry him at age eighteen. Then when I could not continue in a relationship with them, my mother convinced the rest of the family it was my husband and counselor that were turning me against them.

Gaslighting is a form of psychological manipulation that seeks to sow seeds of doubt in a targeted individual or in members of a targeted group, making them question their own memory, perception, and sanity. Gaslighting is a manipulation tactic used to gain power. (16) Believe me, it works very well.

These are the eleven warning signs of gaslighting, used by the narcissist:

They tell blatant lies about you.
They deny they ever said something, even if you have proof.
They use what is near and dear to you as ammunition.
They wear you down over time.
Their actions do not match their words.
They throw in positive reinforcement to confuse you.
They know confusion weakens you.
They project their thoughts and feelings on you.
They align people against you.
They tell you and others that you are the crazy one.
They try to convince you everyone else is a liar. (17)

Narcissists are very good at gaslighting. They have practiced for years and if you are their child you have lived this way your entire life. You don't know any other way. So, when you finally begin to see and hear the truth it's very difficult to break free of the manipulation. However, you must begin the journey of breaking the cycle and healing your emotions. It's not easy to be the cycle breaker. Many people are never able to break away, but if you can, believe me you will not regret it!

For me, once I made the decision to not be controlled any longer and break the cycle of manipulation the road to healing had only just began. After the onslaught of negativity from my family was finally over, the rage inside of me went completely out of control. I have never been that angry. I hated being so angry, but I had to get rid of all the pain and anger I had carried for so long. It was ugly, there is nothing pretty or nice about rage, but if you don't get it out it will turn to bitterness.

Kathy counseled me for two years before I reached a reasonable level of emotional healing. My counseling included hours of talk therapy, reading self-help books, studying and memorizing Scripture, and time, just lots of time.

You cannot rush emotional healing. It takes time; however, now on the other side, I can say that emotional healing is worth the pain and difficulty. Freedom from control of a narcissist and of the self-loathing you've felt your entire life is amazing.

So, if you find yourself in a deep, dark pit or spewing hot lava on the ones you love, search for a companion to walk with you toward freedom. This is not a road you want to walk alone. My children asked me one time, "what is it Miss. Kathy does for you?", my reply, "she's like new glasses, she helps me see things better, clearer." Don't continue simply waiting to see through the fog of manipulation and anger, get new glasses.

CHAPTER 8

The Path to Healing Spiritually

Do You Know the Healer?

The practice of forgiveness is our most important
contribution to healing… —Ellen G. White

O n this journey, I learned that spiritual healing is by far, in
my opinion, the most difficult area to heal. A broken spirit
felt like I would be forever wounded. A broken spirit offers no
hope or perhaps a hair-thin thread you clutch to desperately. The
deep, mortal wound leaves a person wondering, what if this line
breaks, if the hair-thin line breaks, I knew to the very core of my
being, that I would not just fall and be broken, I would shatter.
Like a piece of glass dropped on concrete, laying there in a million
little fragments with no idea how to put myself back together.

When I was in this very precarious situation, all I could do was hang on, hope, and pray for help. When I was not begging God for help, for just a little light so I could see anything good, I was mad, furious even. I was mad at God. I know many of you, probably sitting there with mouth gaping open, thinking you shouldn't be mad at God. I know, I thought the same thing. We just don't get mad at God and if we are, we certainly don't talk about it or tell anyone. But here I am, saying, "I was mad at God."

I even told Him, quite loudly, because I was out of my mind with pain. I didn't know if I was coming or going, crying or screaming, laughing or yelling. My husband, children and I would be sitting at the table enjoying a seemingly normal dinner when I would burst into tears and storm out the door. I would walk for hours, crying and screaming at God, pounding my fists in my pockets. Thinking back now, I'm sure my neighborhood thought I was a mental case. They were right. I was in so much pain spiritually that I was out of my mind.

Coping with physical, emotional, and mental brokenness is nothing compared to having a broken spirit. From a young child, I learned scripture at my grandmother's knee. I went to church with her if I was at her home, which was often. Vacation Bible School, socials, and church functions, we attended them all. We were at the church every time the doors were open. She read the Scripture to me often, taught me hymns, and read me Bible story books for as long as I can remember. I gave my life to Christ and was baptized at six-years of age. My faith ran deep and was strong. That thread of faith, now only small, thin, and tattered, is what held me together.

I had always known where to go when I was hurting. In need of comfort, I would run straight to God, His Word, His Church. That's what I did when my grandmother passed away. She was my lifelong friend, confidant, and source of unconditional love. I thought the worst thing I'd ever go through was losing her. Boy, was I wrong. I had no idea what lay in store for me the next twenty-five years. The ride would get so rough, the brokenness would almost engulf me, and the pain would be almost more than one person could bear.

When your spirit is broken, you are blind. You can't see anything but your own pain and hopelessness. The arrows had come at me from every side piercing my soul, ravaging my mind, shattering my heart, with my pain-filled body rebelling in illness, the arrows pierced me so deeply my soul was split in two. I told God, rather loudly, on all those walks that I was mad at Him. Why did He let this happen? Why had everyone turned on me? Was He next? Why did He put me in that family? Why would He let them hurt me so deeply? Could I even count on Him? The one place I had always gone for comfort. God, His house, His people, didn't even seem to be there for me in my darkest hour. The pain and isolation I felt was almost too much to bear.

I know you may be thinking, you don't talk to God that way. At least that's what I had always thought. You respect God, reverence Him, worship Him, *not* yell at Him. Let me share a little secret that I learned—God is a *BIG* God. He can take your anger, frustration, and pain. Jesus already bore it all on the cross. "Who his own self bare our sins in his own body on the tree, that we, being dead to sins, should live unto righteousness: by whose stripes we were healed." (1 Peter 2:24 KJV)

He experienced anger and He understand how it feels. He even expressed it in scripture. "When it was almost time for the Jewish Passover, Jesus went up to Jerusalem. In the temple courts he found people selling cattle, sheep and doves, and others sitting at tables exchanging money. So, he made a whip out of cords, and drove all from the temple courts, both sheep and cattle; he scattered the coins of the money changers and overturned their tables. To those who sold doves he said, "Get these out of here! Stop turning my Father's house into a market!" His disciples remembered that it is written: "Zeal for your house will consume me." (John 2:13-17 NIV) He even acted on that anger, but He did not sin. "Be ye angry, and sin not: let not the sun go down upon your wrath." (Ephesians 4:26 KJV)

If I had approached my mother and stepdad at this point, I would have sinned. Had I shot someone in anger, I would have sinned. Had I hit my children in my anger, I would have sinned, but I didn't. I just expressed my anger mostly to God, but unfortunately, it spewed on my husband and children from time to time, as well. For that, I feel horrible, have apologized, and ask for their forgiveness.

Once you begin to express that soul brokenness, and get that poisonous anger out, you begin to heal. Healing a broken soul takes time, just like all the steps to healing. It doesn't come easily or quickly, but it will come if you are willing to bare your soul and do the work.

Part of healing your spirit is forgiveness. Forgiveness is *hard*. This was one of the biggest battles for me. I knew from my Christian upbringing, I needed to forgive my family, but I had no idea how. People who have never had their soul absolutely shattered have no idea what this kind of forgiveness entails.

I got plenty of advice, mostly from my Christian friends. Saying, "You know you have to forgive them?" to which my reply would be," *Yes*, I know God calls me to forgive those who have sinned against me, but this is not like someone just cut me off on the highway or who said one hurtful thing to me. This is years and years of blows to my soul that brought me to a point of utter brokenness. You can't possibly understand how deep this pain goes."

As you might have expected, they had no reply. What could they say, until you've experienced this kind of hurt you can't understand.

This kind of forgiveness takes time. It's a process with steps you must go through to get to forgiveness. Most people who haven't experienced such hurt and brokenness can't possibly understand the work it takes to forgive and heal.

What I didn't understand, at the time about forgiveness, is why do I have to forgive them when they don't even think they've done anything to be forgiven for? They don't deserve to be forgiven because they have not repented. How do you forgive such hurt and pain? What are the steps? How do you get there from here?

I knew I wanted to forgive them and that I was supposed to, but I had no idea how to. Like I said, this type of forgiveness is a process requiring time and work. This may come as a surprise to you, but I didn't hate them. I was very angry with them, but I didn't hate them.

The following steps are the process to forgiveness I took:

3 Stages of Forgiveness

Hurt- The first stage is experiencing the hurt. Every time I was hurt, I would try to find a way to forgive and move on. After all, I love these people, they are my family. I wanted everything to be okay and for the hurting to stop. This process for me was hurt, forgive, hurt, forgive, repeat, and repeat for thirty plus years. My personality tends to make me want to be the peacemaker. I strive for peace in every situation, and I would do just about anything to keep the peace. I believe that's why I never told anyone about the sexual abuse I suffered as a child. Telling would have caused more chaos, which wasn't worth it to me. That, along with the feelings of shame and guilt kept me from saying anything.

Hate- At some point the hurt adds up, and you find it harder and harder to forgive. That's when the hurt turns to hate. Yes, *hate*. I didn't see it as hate, but on some level, it was. I honestly didn't want to hate them. Rather, I hated what they did to me, how they treated me, how the situation had turned out, and how they were not in my life anymore, but I didn't hate them. I was angry, and the root of anger is hated and rage. I knew I needed to forgive them and wanted to forgive them, but that was impossible for me at this point.

Again, forgiving is a process. We work through the long-term pain and towards forgiveness, which requires time. I knew I had to make a choice to forgive, and I did eventually forgive them, but it didn't come easily or quickly.

Reaching a place of forgiveness took years, but the good news is choosing forgiveness gets easier with time.

Healing- Finally, Praise God, healing does come. You must understand during this process that God needs you in that place at that time. God does not expect you to forgive overnight, He has his own timing for our healing and doesn't expect us to rush through the process. Even though, like me, you want it over as fast as possible. God simply expects us to allow Him to work in us, and it will happen, if we are willing. Healing is so sweet and such a relief when it finally does come. We begin to see people and situations from a different perspective. We are not looking through the pain, hurt, and anger anymore. Our heart is whole. "And the peace of God, which passeth all understanding, shall keep your hearts and minds through Christ Jesus." (Philippians 4:7 KJV) We feel compassion for those who hurt us because they are still stuck in the hurt, pain, anger, and hate.

You must be willing to study God's word and allow it to permeate every area of your being. God's word is the foundation of healing our spirit. It is truth and light. When you have spent your entire life believing lies, then you let the light of God's word permeate those places and replace the lies with truth, there is freedom and healing like you've never known. For help beginning your spiritual healing you can find a daily devotional in the Companion Guide at ElizabethClamon.com/gift.

I made a point to read scripture daily. I spent many hours in prayer. I listened to praise and worship music. I continued to seek Godly counsel. I chose to totally saturate my life in the light. That's what it took to heal my spirit and it taught me to walk in the light and power of God. Guilt, grief, sadness, fear, and brokenness had saturated me to my core for so long that it took time to let the light of God shine through the cracks. The light becomes brighter as the years of healing continue. Spiritual healing is, in my opinion, the basis for all healing. When our very soul is broken, the only hope of healing is in God.

CHAPTER 9

DONE, The Final Blow
How Many Hits are You Willing to Take?

It is during our darkest moments that we must focus to see the light.—Aristotle Onassis

It's so easy to believe, when you have walked this path, that you are healed, it's *Done*, and you are finished with the brokenness. However, sometimes you can be doing everything that needs to be done to heal and walking in what you believe is freedom, then one thing can cause it all to come back to the surface. You must always be on guard, to protect the progress you've made. Be careful not to be fooled into thinking that because you've healed, the people who contributed to your brokenness have also changed.

I was walking in freedom and gaining healing everyday thinking I was past the worst. Then in a moment it all came crashing back in for me. I received an instant message on Facebook from my aunt. I thought maybe she had a change of heart, maybe she was willing to tell me the truth about my biological father, the thing I still so desperately wanted to know. So, I replied to her message and we chatted for a couple of days and everything seemed fine.

My husband was suspicious, but I thought I could trust her, and my husband went along because he wanted me to be happy.

My aunt asked, "would y'all like to meet us for dinner?", I replied, "sure" hoping that maybe this was the beginning of a new relationship and honesty. By this time, we had been transferred back to Louisiana. We lived about a four-hour drive from her.

I was understandably nervous, my husband suspicious and on guard, but I was hopeful, hopeful that this was the first step to getting my family back and finding out the truth about who my biological father was. That's all I really wanted now, the anger, rage, and guilt gone, I just wanted the truth, reconciliation, and closure.

We met at a popular Italian Restaurant, so that there were lots of people around and it wouldn't be easy to make a big scene. I was always afraid of them causing a big scene and everyone looking at me like I had committed a murder. I was on guard too. Years of heartbreak, disappointment, and my journey back from total brokenness had taught me not to trust them, ever. I guess you could say "trust no one", was my motto. I had lived that way my entire life and something that ingrained in you is hard to change.

We arrived a few minutes early and waited, when my aunt and her husband walked in I was surprised she didn't seem to have changed at all. She was obviously a few years older, but the same and somehow that comforted me. We exchanged greetings and hugs, then came the first blow.

I was fifty pounds heavier, she still as thin as ever, I was walking with a cane and the first thing she said, "Why is your hair so dark!", I thought, What? My hair color, really? My reply

"I colored it", but the truth was my hair had always been black, it was the same color as before I just colored the gray. No mention of the cane or why I had it at just forty-two years old and no mention of my weight gain, that was the comment I was expecting and prepared for.

We were seated, and everything seemed to be going great, polite conversation, good food, very pleasant, and then...as we sat there halfway through our meal she said, "you know your uncle is gone, right?" My mind started racing, what did that mean, why did she say it that way? I just couldn't process what that meant.

My youngest uncle, he was just nine years older than me. He was my favorite, more a big brother, than an uncle. I have fond memories of us playing with toy tractors in the sand pile in my grandmothers' backyard. I thought he could do anything, he could do all kinds of tricks with a yo-yo, ride a unicycle, and from my childlike eyes walk on water. I loved him dearly and missed him terribly through all of this.

As my brain tried to process what she meant by gone, I thought now I know he was having marriage problems, maybe he moved to another state. I looked into her eyes, trying to get some clue as to what gone meant, nothing just a blank stare. So, I ask, "what do you mean, gone?" She looked me right in the eyes, no emotion, no expression, and said, "he's dead".

My mind raced, what, how? How could this be? He was so young, barely in his fifties. Not much older than me. Years of memories flooded my mind, I could not believe this was possible. As tears began to stream down my cheeks, I managed to squeak out, "What? How? When?". It seemed like an eternity as I sat there waiting, but not really wanting the answer. Was this why she had wanted to meet, this was what she wanted to tell me?

Tears flowing down my cheeks like a waterfall now, she looked at me and said, "car accident, a year ago, they think he died immediately, we buried him at mother's feet". No emotion, no compassion, just blunt with an almost hateful tone in her voice. As I sat there, unable to eat, to think, only able to sob quietly, she excused herself to the restroom.

Both our husbands sat there in silence, I continued to sob quietly. When she came back, nothing had changed. She was still emotionless, almost pleased with herself at how badly I was obviously hurting. The rest of our time there was a blur. She told us, "your mother came for the funeral, we are very close now, we even go on vacations together." It was starting to become very clear to me, she had come there to hurt me, stab me in the heart, and she was probably sent by my mother for just that purpose. That's how narcissists behave, if they can't get to you they send a proxy.

The rest of the meal I just sat there and cried, quietly. When we were finished with our meal, we said our goodbyes in the parking lot and went our separate ways. As my husband drove home, I continued to sob, then as the realization of what had just happened to me began to sink in the rage began to surface once again. I thought all that hot lava had been exhausted and I was past those feelings, I was wrong.

I cried for a while, then I got so angry I began punching the dashboard of the car and screaming, the gut-wrenching sound of an animal that is severely wounded with no way to stop the pain. My husband sat silently, not really knowing what to say or do. He told me later that he thought that was it, they had finally hurt me so badly, cut me so deeply, that he was going to have to commit me to a mental hospital.

I went on sobbing, screaming with the gut-wrenching pain and anger, then came silence. I was completely spent, nothing left inside me to get out, I just sat staring out the car window in silence, completely broken, again. They had finally succeeded, they had hurt me so badly there was no emotion left, just emptiness.

When we finally got home, I told my husband, "I'm going to take medicine and go to bed." Again, he just said, "okay" but the look of concern on his face said it all. It was only seven o'clock, I don't take medication to fall asleep, and he was consumed with concern over just how fragile I was. I gave him my phone, so not to be awakened and crawled in bed.

I didn't know anything else until I woke up early the next morning, my husband asleep beside me, my eyes and head throbbing from all the crying. I drug myself out of bed and made my way to the kitchen for a cup of coffee. That's when I saw my cell phone setting on the kitchen table. I picked it up and looked to see if there were calls or texts.

Apparently, several texts had come and gone between my husband and my aunt. She had texted when she got home, it read "we had fun and want to meet y'all again for dinner soon." "*What? Fun!*" I thought. If that was her idea of fun, then they were way sicker than I had even thought. My husband's reply, "I can't believe you would do that to her, just dump that bad news in her lap with no feeling, no compassion, and by the way, congratulations, you may have just pushed her over the edge that she's been fighting for the past seven years. You may have just succeeded in taking her from me forever, I don't know if she can come back, this time."

Her response, "You need to stay out of it, she and I are family and you have nothing to do with this!" He did not respond to that last comment. I'm glad he didn't, because I'm sure his temper would have gotten the best of him.

I sat at the table, coffee in hand, the events of the night before racing through my head. I got the folder that I kept all the letters that had gone back and forth for the last seven years. I read what my mother had written to me, to my middle daughter, to my husband, and the letter from my uncle, my mother's older brother. The venom in those letters and in that text from my aunt was so poisonous it could have killed an elephant. It was coming close to killing me.

I don't know how long I sat there, but at some point, the pain and anger began to subside, and things became very clear to me. They didn't love me; my aunt had only been sent by my mother to hurt me. My mother knew how much I loved my youngest uncle, how bad it would hurt me learning he was gone, and I didn't get to say goodbye or even attend the funeral. Yes, it was crystal clear for the first time, my aunt was sent to stab me in the heart and my mother had given her the knife.

I picked up the phone and sent my last text to them. It read, "you have no right to treat me this way, to hurt me so cruelly, and watch me cry with no compassion in your heart. Tell my mother she doesn't win, the knife she gave you to stab me with is gone, she has no more ability to hurt me, nor do you or any other member of the family. I am done, don't contact me again, and by the way my husband is my family, he's more family to me than any of you have ever been. Goodbye."

I then took the folder that contained all those letters and with a red sharpie I wrote *DONE* across the front. I grieved the loss of my uncle and my family, again. It took a while, but when I was done, I was really done this time. I was finally finished with all the hurt, anger, and guilt, the hot lava finally spent. I could once and for all move forward with my life and learn how to walk-in new-found freedom.

PART 4

HARBOR –
The Where

CHAPTER 10

Living in Sweet Freedom
Are You Ready to be Free?

The question isn't who is going to let me; it's who is
going to stop me.—Ayn Rand

Living in freedom from brokenness is powerful and a sweet
relief, the like of which I've never known. This side of freedom is not always sweet, easy, and smooth sailing. Those learned
thoughts and behaviors have a way of creeping back in if I am not
diligent about being purposeful in putting light in and keeping
darkness out. Habits are hard to break, especially when you have
lived this way for so long. It's easy to slip back into the old habits,
routines, and thoughts you've always had.

I must be diligent in my focus and practices to stay in the
Scriptures and in Prayer. In addition, I only allow people in my
life who edify and encourage me. Am I saying everyone should
walk away from the people who hurt them? No, that was the

right decision for me. Each person must make the right decision as an individual, with much prayer and Godly counsel. You will know the right balance for you in your life, and you must have the courage to act upon what God is leading you to do.

Some people receive healing to the point they can still walk in a relationship with the person who has deeply wounded them. The Holy Spirit gives them the ability to block the harmful words and actions. I was not one of those. I needed a clean break, a fresh start. Being in the process of moving to a new state when all this began was no coincidence.

God needed me to lean and rely on Him solely to receive healing and freedom. Had we not been moving, I would have been inclined to lean on my many friends and seek their council instead of God's wisdom. Friends are wonderful, and I am beyond thankful for the many God has blessed me with. However, during this season of my life I needed to be alone with God. I wasn't totally alone, of course. My husband and children were with me and, of course, I listened to the professional counseling of Kathy, but God didn't need me mucked up in many different opinions and words of wisdom from armchair counselors. He needed me somewhat isolated to walk this path of healing and into freedom.

These years were some of the worst and hardest times of my life and I would never want to repeat them. But, this verse held true for me—"Weeping may endure for a night but joy cometh in the morning." (Psalm 30:5b KJV) My weeping did not last only one night but rather many years because I had much to grieve. Eventually, praise God, joy, healing, and freedom did come. I can't even explain the joy of finally waking up to see a glimpse of light from the bottom of the pit, knowing it was a glimmer of hope and freedom.

Several times during this process I told Kathy, "I just want to quit, it's too hard, it hurts too much, and I just can't do it." I could have done that, just quit. We have a choice and a God-given free will to choose to do or not do anything we want. Kathy said, "Okay, you can quit, but if you quit right now, where will you be tomorrow, next week, next month, or next year? The same place you are now. Nothing will have changed." Wow, Okay. I had been drowning in an awful place, where I was at that moment was not much better, but I want to be free of the pain, so I kept going. *Boy*! Am I ever glad I did.

This side of brokenness is true Joy. I get up every morning now without a million pounds of hurt, anger, and grief on my chest. I can take deep breaths of fresh air. I can turn on music and hear it, as if, for the first time. I rarely think about the people or things that hurt me. I think about my family and I feel compassion for them, not anger and hatred. I pray for them, that they will find a way to get to where I am. I would love nothing more than to see them healed and free of the hurt and pain, but I can't choose that for them. We can only choose for ourselves.

The brokenness no longer stings and hurts. Now a beautiful light shines through the cracks, the light of God and His grace and mercy. I can think back to those times, to the things that broke me, without emotions attached. I don't feel grieved or slighted anymore. I see them for who they are, and they no longer have any power over me. I walk in freedom and know that God is in control. He always has been, and He always will be. The wickedness that I experienced was a result of sin in this world, but the hope He gives us is this, my life verse...

> "And we know that all things work together for good to them that love God, to them who are the called according to his purpose." (Romans 8:28 KJV)

He has worked my terrible experiences for good, because I was called according to His design and purpose. He can, and will use everything, and I mean everything-the good, the bad, the ugly, and the hurtful-for good if you will just be willing to let Him and be His partner in the work. Allowing Him to work in His time is not easy, I would never tell you it was, but nothing is sweeter than freedom.

> "To appoint unto them that mourn in Zion, to give unto them beauty for ashes, the oil of joy for mourning, the

garment of praise for the spirit of heaviness; that they might be called trees of righteousness, the planting of the LORD, that he might be glorified." (Isaiah 61:3 KJV)

Conclusion

Remember no one can make you feel inferior without
your consent.—Eleanor Roosevelt

Everyone walks through brokenness; at least everyone I've ever met
has some brokenness. Brokenness sometimes come in an instant
with a look, a word, or even something unspoken that hurts, or
like in my case, brokenness builds over time and repeated injury
to the point when life cannot continue as is.

Regardless of how broken you feel, how long it took to get
to where you are, or how far away wholeness seems, there is
hope. When you are at the bottom of the pit of brokenness and
despair sometimes hope is all there is to hold on to. At least that
was the case for me. From the pit of despair, illness, depression,
anger, all I had to hold on to was hope, hope that if I continued
to press forward and into God, I could somehow find healing
and wholeness.

I wanted out of the brokenness so bad I would have done just
about anything to get out of the pit of despair. I tried running,

crawling, fighting, screaming, and yelling, but healing comes slowly. Healing takes persistence, patience, long-suffering and time. As bad as you want it to be over it won't be over until God's perfect timing.

How long healing took was a very hard concept for me. I have always had a strong work ethic, one of many coping mechanisms I'm sure. I know very well how to put my head down, push hard and get through whatever needs to be done. I come from a long line of very independent, stubborn, self-sufficient, hard-working women, who do whatever must be done to get things done. I naturally thought this was the way to get through this process as well. I was so wrong.

I prayed through this entire process, "God, what do You want me to do?". The only answer I got repeatedly was, "Be still, and know that I am God: I will be exalted among the heathen, I will be exalted in the earth." (Psalm 46:10 KJV) God could have told me to cut off my head and it would have been easier for me. But God in all His infinite wisdom knew how hard being still was for me. He knew exactly what He was asking of me, which was, for me, near impossible. The only way I could be still and get through the brokenness was total dependence on Him.

It was a time for me to learn to be still, to commune with God, without distraction, and to learn not to occupy myself with busyness just to keep myself from the dealing with the pain inside me. I had always used busyness to keep from facing my brokenness and now I had to learn to be still and work through the hurt. I wasn't very good at being still and sometimes when we can't get a concept, we must learn it the hard way.

Is my healing complete? *No*, I don't know if you ever completely heal from such deep and utter brokenness. What I do know is God is working in you a might work. He has given you a calling, and if you're willing you will see His plan come into focus. I also know that everything, and I mean everything you go through is preparing you for the next thing.

Because I wouldn't be still, I had to learn the hard way: "Be still and know that I am God: I will be exalted among the heathen, I will be exalted in the earth." (Psalm 46:10 KJV)

84

What happens when your worst fears become reality?
Take the next step in your journey by reading and excerpt from my next book.

Shattered; Rise from the Pieces and Rebuild your Life

Be still and know that I am God. The words I kept hearing when I prayed what do you want me to do now? I would like to say I waited patiently for an answer, but I seldom wait patiently for anything. I had put in thirty-eight years moving. Always moving to get ahead of the pain, the anger, the inability to understand why things had happened the way they did. Now, after all the struggle and turmoil I had gone through God wanted me to be still. "*What*? "I protested, "God, I don't understand, nor do I know how to be still."

Just three years earlier, in 2002, before my near nervous breakdown, God had called me to speak and share my story with those who are struggling in the midst of a difficult family situation. At first, I thought it was my imagination, but then the youth pastor's wife stopped me after church the next Sunday and said, "at that conference the women's group went to I thought about you. You would be really good at speaking like that, with all your experiences moving with the military and homeschooling your children." I replied, "Thank you" more than a little stunned that maybe it wasn't my imagination.

We left that day after church. We were moving to our next duty station and I had only just begun the journey of *Beauty Rising from Brokenness*. One night on the five-day trip to our next duty station I was reading my devotional, what I read was...

"See, I have made him a witness to the peoples, a ruler and commander of the peoples. Surely you will summon nations you know not, and nations you do not know will come running to you, because of the Lord your God, the Holy One of Israel, for he has endowed you with splendor." (Isaiah 55: 4-5)

The devotional was about God calling you to spread His word. It felt like God was speaking directly to me, affirming what I heard at the conference, from the youth pastor's wife, and now here it was right in front of me in Scripture. God was calling me into ministry, how exciting. Little did I know what lay ahead, I had to resolve the turmoil inside of me from the childhood traumas and the chronic illnesses that developed due to it. However, I had a calling something to work towards, a goal. I love goals and list and laying out orderly steps to take to accomplish something. Boy! How naïve was I?

First came the long hard journey from Brokenness, three years of anger, rage, broken-heartedness, then just as I was regaining my life, getting on my feet, ready to run again towards this calling came Shattered....

I was feeling much better, my health stabilized, my energy levels up, and coming back to myself. In a couple of weeks, we were going to a family reunion with my husband's family and I was feeling invincible. The children and I missed home, Louisiana, so much we decided to leave a week and a half early and go visit friends before the family reunion. I would take the two younger children and drive from Michigan to Louisiana, visit our friends and my husband's family, then drive back and met my husband and our oldest daughter in Kentucky for the camping family reunion.

We met them, along with my in-laws, who were working on a church in northern Michigan that summer, my sisters-in-law and their families for three days of camping, swimming, and boating.

We had a great time just enjoying each other's company. Friday finally came, and it was time for everyone to head their separate way.

After all the goodbyes we all struck out for our next destination. My in-laws were about an hour ahead of us, headed back to Michigan to work on a church. They were part of a missionary team that traveled in their RV's repairing and building churches. We headed out, ready to get home and back to normal life. I was thrilled not to have to do anymore driving. I was quite tired of driving, so I kicked back in the front seat of the suburban to read. My husband driving, pulling the fully loaded camper, and our sixteen and eighteen-year-old daughters driving the truck following us. It was a nice day, hot for July in Michigan, but good to be headed home.

A couple hours into the drive we suddenly had a blowout on the camper. We pulled over and changed the tire and got back on the road. My husband knew all the tires on the camper being the same age, there was a good chance we could have another blowout, so he drove in the far-right lane, just in case we needed to pull off the highway again.

About six miles before we crossed the Michigan border we began to see the all too familiar signs warnings of road construction ahead. There's a running joke in Michigan that there are just two seasons, winter and construction. The signs instructed all semi-trucks to drive in the left-hand lane. In the construction area the lanes shifted to the shoulder of the road and the right lane. However, the semi-truck in front of us was not obeying the signs for some reason. He continued to drive in the right lane, which was the shoulder of the road.

My phone rang, it was my mother-in-law, wanting to know how close we were to home. They had stopped at the campground on the military base for the night and were waiting on us to go to dinner. I told her we would be home in about forty-five minutes and we would love to go to dinner. Our eleven-year-old son sitting in the backseat of the suburban watching movies asked, "where does grandma want to go to dinner?" I turned around to answer his question, as I answered I saw something out of the corner of my eye that didn't quite register in my brain.

My husband was stomping on the break with both feet as hard as he could. My mind, dazed and confused, thought you can't stop the camper like that. After eight years of pulling this camper all over the United States, moving with the military, that much I knew. I managed to turn my head just enough to see the front of the suburban about to make impact with the bumper of the semi-truck in front of us.

Then just the sound of crushing metal, the smell of smoke, and the bloodcurdling screams of my son. I was so disoriented I couldn't figure out how to unbuckle my seatbelt, how to get the door open, or how get to my son. My mind raced, what had just happened? I couldn't put the pieces together, where were we, what was going on? Then I heard a phone ringing, I need to answer that, but where is it? I can't find it. My brain, nor my body could make any sense of this, what had just happened?

APPENDICES

Acknowledgements

Special Thanks to:

Marci Young for your editing and input to make this book become a reality

Proofreading provided by Mark Schultz at Wordrefiner.com

Endnotes

Introduction:

(1) A practical guide to Naturopathy Steward Mitchell
(2) Linda Page's Healthy Healing 12th Edition

Chapter 1: Brokenness, How did I Get Here?

(3) Publishing: © 2017 Atlas Music Publishing / House Of
     Story Music Publishing / Two Story House Music / Highly
     Combustible Music (ASCAP) / Housermania Music/
     (ASCAP) (admin. by Amplified Administration) [emphasis
     added] Writer(s): Jason Houser, AJ Pruis and Matthew West
(4) https://ukhealthcare.uky.edu/wellness-community/
     news-events/health-information/
     short-and-long-term-effects-preterm-birth

     *This article first appeared in the Huffington Post. Donna
     Jackson Nakazawa is the author of Childhood Disrupted:
     How Your Biography Becomes Your Biology and How you
     Can Heal.*

(5)   http://www.health.state.mn.us/divs/cfh/program/ace/index.cfm
(6)   https://acestoohigh.com/2016/08/10/childhood-trauma-leads-to-lifelong-chronic-illness-so-why-isnt-the-medical-community-helping-patients/

Chapter 5: The Path to Healing Physically

(7)   http://beba.org/early-traum/
(8)   https://my.clevelandclinic.org/health/articles/11874-stress
(9)   http://www.nucdf.org/documents/OxidativeStress.pdfhttps://
(10) https://english.stackexchange.com/questions/102939/what-is-a-canary-in-a-coal-mine
(11) https://www.naturalhealers.com/massage-therapy/history/

Chapter 7: Path to Healing Emotionally

(12) www.health.harvard.edu/blog/tai-chi-can-improve-life-for-people-with-chronic-health-conditions-201509248349
(13) emotions definition Safari online dictionary
(14) https://simple.m.wikipedia.org/wiki/List_of_emotions
(15) https://www.psychologytoday.com/us/blog/communication-success/20160 2/10-signs-narcissistic-parent
(16) https://en.m.wikipedia.org/wiki/Gaslighting
(17) https://www.psychologytoday.com/us/blog/here-there-and-everywhere/20170 1/11-warning-signs-gaslighting

IF YOU LIKED THE BOOK YOU WILL LOVE
THE EXPERIENCE

You can work with Elizabeth directly. Elizabeth can guide you through the journey to healing and wholeness through The *Beauty Rising from Brokenness* coaching program that will take you down the path to healing physically, mentally, emotionally, and spiritually.

> "Imagine what your life would be like if you made the choice to take your brokenness, walk through the traumas that broke you, and turned those into the healthy, whole life you've been dreaming of?"

You can join Elizabeth's signature coaching programs Beauty Rising from Brokenness, her event held twice a year, participate in the online course, or join her online support community Beauty Rising from Brokenness on Facebook. Participants can join from anywhere in the world.

More information Here: ElizabethClamon.com/coach

Don't stay in your Brokenness, make the choice to heal and be free today.

Join us at

THE BEAUTY RISING FROM BROKENNESS

Live Event

Imagine hearing straight from Elizabeth and spending a weekend working with her and her team to Gain Freedom from Brokenness

Everyone learns differently, and many studies show that experiencing a live event reaches you on a deeper level. You can engage all your senses to absorb the most value from the training.

Join us for our Live Event held twice a year. Where you will hear others experiences of Beauty Rising from Brokenness, you'll work directly with Elizabeth on healing the traumas that began your journey and get started on the path to healing.

INVEST IN YOURSELF and YOUR HEALTH by TAKING THE NEXT STEP TO FREEDOM FROM BROKENNESS

FIND OUT MORE AT ElizabethClamon.com/event

THE BEAUTY RISING FROM BROKENNESS
COMPANION GUIDE

Get the FREE Companion Guide to help you on your journey to

BEAUTY RISING FROM BROKENNESS

Comes with assessments, guides, devotionals, and tips and tricks to help you begin the journey to become healed, whole and free from Brokenness

Get your Companion Guide at ElizabethClamon.com/gift

Speaker, Author, Coach

HAVE ELIZABETH COME SPEAK

Elizabeth is a professional speaker who is sought after to share her message all over the world. She understands the importance of finding the right speaker with the right message for your group or event. Elizabeth speaks on a variety of topics from natural healing, wellness, leadership, and empowerment. She knows the success of any event can hinge on the getting the right speaker and she commits to make your event a premier event for you and your audience.

Elizabeth is engaging, entertaining, and energetic in her delivery. She will take your audience on a one of a kind uplifting experience that they will never forget. She is keenly aware of the need to engage an audience and connect on an emotional level. She will equip your audience with key takeaways and a new perspective on how to live their life Relentlessly. She customizes her message and trainings to achieve and exceed your expectations and desired goals.

Contact Elizabeth today to begin a conversation on how she may serve you and your audience Elizabethclamon.com

**Elizabeth donates a portion of all her earnings
to Military Spouse Organizations.**

As a military spouse for thirty years Elizabeth understands the unique needs of military spouses whose service member is deployed or no longer with them. She has spent many years supporting military spouses' organizations and chooses to support them with a donation of every sale.

About The Author

Elizabeth M. Clamon, is living proof that natural healing and the power of prayer works. She lives in North Carolina with her husband and his six cats. She is an avid reader, researcher, DNA sleuth, Cajun cook, and motorcycle enthusiast.

She has not only survived, but thrived, despite childhood abuse, being chronically ill, and left disabled and bedridden for twelve years from an auto accident. She provides an insightful, inspirational, and educational experience to inspire people to overcome obstacles and live their dreams.

Elizabeth studied Holistic Nutrition and Naturopathic Medicine at Clayton College of Health. She also studied psychology at Louisiana Baptist University.

She is a business owner, professional speaker, Amazon best-selling author, coach, and consultant who works with clients to heal physically, mentally, emotionally, and spiritually. She brings a unique perspective when she speaks, by not only sharing her twenty-two years of experience in the health and wellness field, but also her experience as a chronic pain patient, military spouse, homeschool mother, and survivor of childhood trauma.

Elizabeth loves to empower people, help them gain valuable information on how to take an obstacle and use it for good to overcoming trauma, and adversity with actionable steps that can be taken immediately to pursue living their life to be relentless in the pursuit of your health, passion and purpose, so that they can not only survive, but thrive, enabling them to live their best life.

Connect with Elizabeth at: ElizabethClamon.com